DYING

The Power of Forgiveness

TO LIVE

Harold L. Senkbeil

CPH™
SAINT LOUIS

1 2 3 4 5 6 7 8 9 10   02 01 00 99 98 97 96 95 94 93

Let this be recorded for a generation to come
so that a people yet unborn may praise the LORD.

Psalm 102:18 RSV

To three special people, who are their parents' joy and pride:
Michael Leigh Senkbeil
Katherine Jane Senkbeil
Timothy Nesset Senkbeil

Dying to live, God grant you life in all its abundance
in Him who is our Life.

Contents

To Start With

"The church is a mouth-house," Martin Luther once said, "not a pen-house."

"Christ himself wrote nothing," he continued, "nor did he give command to write, but to preach orally."

By vocation I am a preacher, and I know what Luther was talking about. Words ring in the ear differently than they appear on a page. The living voice of the Gospel loses something when muffled by ink and print.

That's why sitting down to write about doctrine is risky. The sacred mysteries of the faith always suffer under dissection. Cold description won't do; these truths call for lively dialog. No doubt that's why the Wittenberg reformer—himself a prolific author—so highly prized the verbal interchange of fellow Christians. "Mutual conversation and consolation of brethren," he called it.

The words on the following pages are half of my "mutual conversation" with you. A mutual journey, actually—a kind of joint pilgrimage.

In writing *Sanctification: Christ in Action* (Milwaukee: Northwestern Publishing House, 1989), I outlined a Lutheran response to the challenge mounted by American evangelical Christianity at the close of the 20th century. There I described a personal pilgrimage into the heritage of the Lutheran church—a Christian life rooted in the objective realities of the Incarnation, the Word, and the Sacraments.

This book covers much of the same terrain, but without the academic luggage I carried last time. Since I'm traveling lighter, I hope the living voice of the Gospel speaks more clearly through these printed words. If so, I know our conversation will provide some consolation for you.

As my travel companion, please don't be alarmed by the "Lutheran" label on the hiking garb. I hope to offer something for your own journey, no matter what label you wear. Lutherans, you see, have always held their doctrine to be both thoroughly evangelical and genuinely catholic. Far from a 16th century novelty, the Lutheran confessors saw their faith as nothing more than a summary of what Christians always and everywhere had believed: "the ancient consensus which the universal and orthodox church of Christ has believed, fought for against many heresies and errors, and repeatedly affirmed" (Preface to the Book of Concord, 1580). That "ancient consensus" and its application to the Christian life—its "so what?"—was the focus last time around.

This book is really an excursion into the "now what?" of the Christian life, and that means it's no armchair travelog. I speak as one traveler to another. You could be a life-long Christian or a novice in the faith; perhaps you're just curious. But no matter. For we're fellow pilgrims, you and I. The road gets rough now and then. But it is Christ's road. And that makes all the difference in the world.

Harold L. Senkbeil
All Saints Day 1993

Where Credit Is Due . . .

A book as conscientiously conversational as this one leans heavily on prior conversations. At the back of this volume I have listed some of the books which have been formative for me, but it would be impossible to list all the people who were important conversation partners. Still, there are certain individuals who deserve special thanks. Without them this book would not have taken shape as it did.

My first thanks go to my wife, Jane Nesset Senkbeil, for her help along the way. It's tough enough being a pastor's wife—but when he takes up writing, the challenge is multiplied. Jane managed the adjustment with both grace and good humor—one of her unique gifts. She helped me carve out time for this project and provided important feedback to the material as it took shape. She indeed lives up to her name: Jane is God's gift to me.

Special thanks are also due Dr. Robert Kolb, whose *Speaking the Gospel Today: A Theology for Evangelism* (CPH, 1984) first captured my imagination on the central Biblical themes of life and death. Despite heavy teaching and research responsiblities, he faithfully read each of the chapters as I completed them. His critique was eagerly anticipated, and his enthusiasm proved contagious, giving me renewed energy to continue.

It always helps to have someone keep you on target. University Lutheran Chapel, Minneapolis, Minn., provided needed "target practice." During the writing process, members of University Lutheran Chapel field-tested the manuscript in their book study group. My thanks to these young men and women for their help and to their pastor, the Rev. John Pless, for his encouraging words.

"As iron sharpens iron," Solomon wrote, "so one man sharpens another" (Prov. 27:17). This book has a sharper edge because of a very patient friend, Edward Treptow. He waded through the developing manuscript line by line; the result is a more penetrating book.

9

The themes which find voice in these words were first sharpened in our mutual conversation—my brother's help and consolation are gratefully acknowledged.

ALMIGHTY GOD, the giver of all good things, without whose help all Labour is ineffectual, and without whose grace all wisdom is folly, grant, I beseech Thee, that in this my undertaking, thy Holy Spirit may not be withheld from me, but that I may promote thy glory, and the Salvation both of myself and others; grant this, O Lord, for the sake of Jesus Christ. Amen.

From *Dr. Johnson's Prayers*, Elton Trueblood, ed. [Dublin, Ind.: Prinit Press, 1981], p. 7.

PART I

The Incarnational Foundation of the Christian Life

1

Our Dying World

...in Adam all die. (1 Cor. 15:22)

"This looks good," she thought to herself. Such shiny fruit; it fairly cried out to be eaten, to be enjoyed. And what a broadening experience such enjoyment would be—the knowledge of good and evil, the Mighty One had said. How could He want less than the very best for His own? "My husband and I will be like God Himself," she reflected. "Now, could that be so bad?" The serpent made sense: it would be much better to know both good and evil than to know only good.

"Here, have some." She handed the juicy pulp to her husband. "This is good stuff.

"By the way, Adam, do you know what He meant by that word—I think it was die?"

Our Predicament

Where are we headed? Everybody wants to know, but strangely enough we're not asking. Most of us are too busy with other questions: questions such as "How can we defend ourselves against terrorism?" "Was the nuclear holocaust nightmare just a bad dream?" "When is the next international crisis coming?" "What about the AIDS epidemic?"

Or maybe other questions: "Will my contract be renewed when I come up for review?" "Will I be able to keep up the mortgage payments?" "Will my children survive the perils of adolescence?"

Or maybe more personal questions: "Why am I empty inside much of the time?" "Why did my mother die?" "Why does my best friend have cancer?"

You may have still other questions. The details really don't matter. For finally all questions boil down to one central issue: Where are we headed in this world of ours?

PART I: THE INCARNATIONAL FOUNDATION

As the 20th century draws to a close and the third millennium of the Christian era looms large, this old world of ours is filled with a confusing mixture of hope and despair. On the one hand, great optimism and confidence in expanding technology, and yet on the other, perplexing fear and anxiety over the unknown.

One thing's for sure. We're all DYING TO LIVE. We'd like to have our crack at life, and we'd give anything to taste everything it has to offer. But we know it won't last. Ultimately, all of life is lived graveside. We are all dying—from the youngest newborn to the oldest nursing-home resident. We might be dying to live, but we're all dying.

That's our predicament as human beings on planet earth. All other issues, from the win/loss record of the local Little League team to the international war on drugs, fade in comparison. There's only one bottom line in this world of ours: Death.

Our Moral Crisis

The entertainment world has come a long way since Rhett Butler uttered the first *damn* on the silver screen. Television and movie producers scramble to find enough titillation to grab the attention of an increasingly jaded audience. Under the guise of authenticity, viewers are treated to graphic scenes of torture and dismemberment, illicit sex and perversion.

Some would lay the blame for our declining morals on the doorstep of filmmakers and TV producers. But the media aren't to blame any more than bathroom mirrors cause our pimples and wrinkles. The entertainment industry simply reflects the moral climate of our age. The source of the problem is elsewhere. In the immortal words of the cartoon character Pogo: "We have met the enemy and he is us."

Too often we look to the world around us as the source of our moral problem. If we could just stamp out pornography, we think, we could get rid of sexual abuse. If we could clean up the lyrics to rock music we could solve the drug problem. But these are really only the symptoms of a much more drastic predicament.

Of course these issues do deserve our attention; we need to clean up the cesspool. But remember, cesspools aren't the source of sewage. Neither is the world the source of sin. The cause of moral pollution, Jesus said, is found much closer to home:

> "What goes into a man's mouth does not make him 'unclean,' but what comes out of his mouth, that is what makes him 'unclean.' . . . Don't you see that whatever enters the mouth goes into the stomach and then out of the body? But the things that come out of the mouth come from the heart, and these make a man 'unclean.' For out of the heart come evil thoughts, murder, adultery, sexual immorality, theft, false testimony, slander." (Matt. 15:11, 17–19)

This is strong language. It's tough to take. Reality is sometimes hard to stomach. And this is one reality we need to face head on: every last one of the horrifying sins in the world outside can be found inside our own hearts. This ugly truth is crucial in addressing the moral crisis of our age. If Christians are to have any lasting impact on the world at the end of the 20th century, we'll have to address the real problem. We must attack the cause, not merely the symptoms.

Let's take a look at the real source of our moral quandary. Let me warn you, it's not a pretty picture. The filthy atmosphere of our age is nauseating enough, but the real problem goes deeper. The ugly fact is, we ourselves add to the pollution. Our nostrils might be offended by the smell of our moral climate, but we need to sniff more carefully. A stench filters out of our own pores. It is the stench of death.

A World in Crisis

To all appearances, our world seems increasingly godless. And godlessness must be the problem, we think. If the world could be more religious, we would solve our moral crisis. However, maybe the problem isn't the godlessness of our age, but rather the gods of our age.

St. Paul's description of the sophisticated Athenians applies just as well today: *"I see that in every way you are very religious"* (Acts 17:22). He then proceeded to describe the idols he had observed in their city, including the altar inscribed "To an unknown god."

This "unknown god," he claimed, had made himself known in Jesus Christ.

That's not a bad mission strategy, and it could serve Christians well in proclaiming the Gospel in our own day. But first we have to get rid of the idea that we live in a godless world.

In his Large Catechism, Martin Luther wrote: "A god is that to which we look for all good and in which we find refuge in every time of need." By that definition our world is anything but godless. It's just that we have manufactured our own gods.

Materialism has been the whipping boy of the Christian church in the western world for decades, and not without cause. Material things do have a tendency to blind people to spiritual realities. And the search for "stuff," as we call the merchandise of this world, has become an international obsession. Eastern Europe and the Third World are developing an insatiable appetite for the goods that have defined "the good life" in the West. We all have to admit it: material things tend to become "that to which we look for all good"

But I wonder if the problem doesn't run deeper. Maybe our problem is the plastic toyland we live in.

The Plastic Toyland

The issue of materialism comes into focus when we remember Jesus' words: "What goes into a man's mouth does not make him 'unclean,' but what comes out of his mouth, that is what makes him 'unclean.'" That is to say, it's not the material things of this world that are the issue, but our attitude toward those things.

Jesus warned his disciples about the pitfall of wealth in His comical comparison between the rich man entering heaven and a camel trying to squeeze through the eye of a needle. The real problem wasn't the riches, Jesus was saying, but the rich man. It wasn't what the rich man owned, but what owned him. In other words, it was a First Commandment issue: here was a man with the wrong god.

Christians at the dawn of the 21st century are faced with plenty of alternatives to the real God of heaven and earth. But I would suggest that the chief false god of our age is pleasure.

Not long ago people found happiness even when they had little or no pleasure. Happiness was viewed not as an end in itself, but as a by-product of relationships forged on the anvil of family, friends, and vocation. Now, however, the focus seems to have changed. Thomas Jefferson wrote of the right to "the pursuit of happiness." Americans at the end of the 20th century seem blind to this conditional view of happiness. We have rewritten the Declaration of Independence; we now see happiness as an inherent right. And we have also redefined happiness. No longer is it the result of relationships and work. We *demand* happiness. We want it now, and we want it on our terms and according to our own definition: personal pleasure.

You don't have to look at lifestyles to see this change; our language gives us away. Americans increasingly communicate with "I" talk. "I think" has been replaced by "I feel." "I would like" has given way to "I want." In each example the second "I" is bigger than the first. In "I" talk, the self speaks in louder and louder tones until rational thought is drowned out in emotion.

Increasingly people are less and less concerned with truth and more and more concerned with pleasure. Despite the move toward health foods, hamburgers are packaged and sold with an eye toward satisfying our taste buds more than our dietary needs. "You deserve a break today" and "Have it your way" have been successful sales pitches, but they could just as well be slogans for our age.

You and I live in a "me first" era. We're conditioned to have it our way; we're told to have whatever we want. And we're told in no uncertain terms what we should want: whatever pleases us, pure and simple. Surprisingly, instead of resisting what amounts to blatant propaganda, we buy into this package. It seems perfectly obvious to most people that life should be focused on personal pleasure.

No wonder, then, that increasing chunks of our time and energy are given over to toys: activities and things designed primarily to give us pleasure. The satirical bumper sticker of the '80s is turning out to be a prophetic description of the '90s: WHOEVER DIES WITH THE MOST TOYS WINS.

And that's just the problem, isn't it? The world we live in is a toyland. The things we are told will bring us pleasure are just things;

they have no happiness to give in themselves. Their promise is an empty promise; no possession or activity comes with happiness attached.

The Old Testament preacher said it long ago:

> I have seen all the things that are done under the sun; all of them are meaningless, a chasing after the wind. . . . I denied myself nothing my eyes desired; I refused my heart no pleasure. My heart took delight in all my work, and this was the reward for all my labor. Yet when I surveyed all that my hands had done and what I had toiled to achieve, everything was meaningless, a chasing after the wind; nothing was gained under the sun. (Eccl. 1:14; 2:10–11)

Sadly, the world goes on chasing after the wind as the clock winds down. It is a world of glitz and glitter, but it's just a toyland. Ultimately, even people with the most toys must die.

Plastic People

As people look for something real in a world of plastic, they reach out to others. This is as it should be, for the Creator of heaven and earth has made humans in His own image. In part, being created in God's image means we have a built-in need for fellowship; we aren't designed to go solo in this life. We were made to live in mutually satisfying harmony with our neighbors on planet earth. But tragically, we frequently find dissonance instead of harmony.

Reaching out to others, too often we run into a wall of isolation or rejection. We ask a colleague for help, and she ignores us. We gather our courage to reveal our true feelings to a friend, and he nervously changes the subject. These walls are built for self-defense; to one degree or another we all sense a need to protect ourselves from others' demands. Sometimes it's out of fear, sometimes out of frustration. Yet it feels like the same thing to the person on the outside looking in: loneliness.

Rising crime rates have frightened merchants and homeowners alike. We reflect a fortress mentality. Business is good for bullet-proof glass manufacturers. Not only the sheriff's receptionist, but also gas-station attendants sit behind barriers of steel and glass, hermetically sealed against intruders. New homes and condos are built to screen and seal people from the outside world. Once front porches invited passers-by to sit and chat; now our garages shield us from our neighbors, and we sit securely in climate-controlled environments until it's time to venture out again in our motorized cubicles. Once we practiced the fine art of communication, that most delicate balance between words, posture, and expression by which human beings open their hearts to each other. Now we are increasingly content to be entertained by shadowy electronic images on video screens.

Such is life in the real world, we say. But it's not real. It's a plastic world we've made for ourselves, populated with plastic people. And we pay a great price for all this plastic. For when you get right down to it, beneath all the busyness and hype of our daily routine, we lead lonely lives. We've walled ourselves off from reality; we've convinced ourselves that plastic will do and counterfeit is good enough. But it's not. Underneath the surface we still have a deep hunger for reality. The desperate longing of human hearts to unload their joys and sorrows to one another is dimly echoed in the empty chatter of celebrity talk shows. But it's a pretty cheap imitation. And, if you listen closely, you can hear something under all this trivial chatter. It is the voice of a profound emptiness in our culture, which has settled for plastic instead of reality. It is the voice of despair. It's really the empty echo of our own voice; for, each in our own way, you and I too cry out from the death in which we live.

The Loneliness Epidemic

Most Americans would tell you they have no time to be lonely. From dawn until the wee hours of the night, we jam our schedules with the myriad of activities we call living. *And besides,* we like to think, *how can we be lonely if we're around so many people so much of the time?* In fact, we probably think our real problem is not loneliness, but too much togetherness. Like the late Hollywood recluse, Greta Garbo, we cherish our privacy. "I vant to be alone" is our motto, too.

And so we settle for surface talk that keeps people at a distance. "How are you today?" greets the checkout clerk, not really wanting to know. "Just fine, thanks," we reply, not wanting to let him know either. We paste on our plastic grin as he hands over our change with an obligatory "Have a nice day." "You too," we say pleasantly, our thoughts actually a million miles away.

Surface talk is all right once in a while; indeed it's vital at times. But as a steady diet it leaves us decidedly empty, even starved. We learn to cover up our real thoughts and to bail out of conversations when they get too uncomfortable with a casual "You know what I mean." But how could anyone know unless we tell them? When we keep our true feelings to ourselves, no one really knows what we mean. Now if that's not loneliness, what is it?

We claim to have lots of friends. But what we call "friends" are mostly acquaintances. We work with them; we play with them; we eat with them; we drink with them; we chat with them. But what we don't do is talk with them. Not really. Somehow we've learned to keep our guard up when we're around other people. "That way we won't get burned," we tell ourselves. We're afraid to risk being honest—it takes too much energy, and it leaves us too vulnerable. What will that person think of me if I share my fears or weaknesses? And what could he do with that information?

That's why we keep our true feelings to ourselves. It's better that way, we think, because then we won't have to be bothered with anyone else's problems either. "I've had to handle my life; let him deal with his own problems" is our attitude. And still we call them "friends." But they're not. In fact, they're not a whole lot different than the images on our TV screens: busy, chattering, entertaining— but not real. Real friends are more than that.

And so we look for surrogate friends. We hire a therapist we can pay to keep our deepest feelings in confidence. We join a support group, certain that no one in the group will "rat" on us; all of us have too much to lose. Now counselors and support groups are much better than no help at all, that's for sure. But when you think about it, confidentiality based on money or intimidation is a pretty poor substitute for real friendship.

As a nation, we're reading prodigious quantities of books about gaining friends and keeping them. We have a genuine hunger for meaningful friendships; we're just too busy, we tell ourselves. But the truth is, we're not willing. Not really. It's too risky. And so we live alone in a sea of togetherness. We're drowning in chatter while thirsting for talk—real talk from one human heart open to another. I'd call that loneliness, wouldn't you?

And loneliness is a big problem for human beings as the 21st century dawns. In fact, it's a regular epidemic; an epidemic of loneliness in our dying world.

The Information Age

We're victims of our own technology. In rural societies whole families once lived and worked together; neighbors depended on each other for their living and their very lives. Raising animals and growing crops, men and women had something to show for their labor. They found satisfaction and fulfillment in their work. They could see the fruits of their labor in their barns and granaries, not just in their bank accounts. It was the same in cottage industries: artisans worked in their own homes, turning out useful and finely crafted items with pride. With the dawning of industrialization, however, fathers left home for work, with nothing to show when they returned except a paycheck. Work began to be an end in itself instead of a means of producing necessary goods. Job satisfaction began a steep decline. Over the last century and a half that's the way it's been in America.

Now we see a new phenomenon. Technology has amplified the problem and further altered the home and the workplace alike. Business is increasingly geared to the marketing of information, which is even less tangible than goods mass-produced on the assembly line. And now it's not just fathers going off to work: mothers and teenagers all have their own jobs, too. And when they return home, they've got nothing to show for it except money. And frustration. And exhaustion. And loneliness.

For loneliness is an occupational hazard in the workaday world. True enough, on the job, we're with people much of the time. And we're told we're a valuable part of the team. But we can see right through that. We know most of that talk about teamwork is just talk. The truth is, at work we're all rivals. Every one of us is a potential candidate for promotion—and when that time comes, teamwork won't count for much. Mostly, it'll be a matter of how we've performed. And so we perform because we know we have to in order to save our own necks. It's all part of having an edge over other people. And it might make for promotions. But it doesn't do much for friendships.

We're moving faster and faster, but we don't seem to be getting anywhere. We're more "successful," but we're less satisfied. For the god of pleasure will never be satisfied. No matter how many plastic toys we accumulate or how many plastic people we move among, the god of pleasure demands still more. "Have it your way," is his insistent plea. But we never have it our way, not entirely.

And so we move from job to job and city to city, looking for satisfaction and fulfillment. But we have no roots. And so we have no friends. Not real friends, anyway, or precious few of them. Is it any wonder we lead lonely lives at the end of the 20th century?

The Love Famine

Even the closest of human relationships are under attack these days. Divorce rates skyrocket, families break apart, and children are raised by one parent or by the parent's new spouse. Many children are raised by people who don't really "raise" them at all. And so the ugly cycle repeats itself: anger, bitterness, and more anger. Alarming numbers of children grow up with no place they can really call home, no safe place where they can learn what it means to love and to be loved. And these children grow up to be adults who don't know how to give and receive love.

Can you grasp the depth of this self-perpetuating tragedy? You can fill a food-starved stomach, after all; but how do you heal a love-starved soul? Worse yet, how can a person love anyone else if the word means nothing to him? We have a nice clinical phrase to describe this social disaster. We call it "dysfunctional families." But what it adds up to is brokenness. And under that brokenness is sin. And under that sin lies death.

The AIDS epidemic has people running scared as the '90s begin. But the potential impact of the loneliness epidemic is just as scary. Hundreds of thousands of people in our age have never learned to love. And I'm not talking only about friendships; why else do couples move from relationship to relationship, and from bed to bed, if not because of this loneliness epidemic?

The Sexual Disaster

God designed men and women to share in the closest of all human relationships, the strongest bond, the most intimate human union—marriage. This union is expressed in sexual intercourse, which the Bible describes as "knowing." From our viewpoint today, when sex is widely considered to be essentially a mechanical bodily function, that word seems a little quaint, just the sort of thing you'd expect from old-fashioned prudes who blush to speak directly about sex. But it's no euphemism. Rather, "knowing" accurately describes sex as it really is: intimate disclosure of body, heart, and soul. Now, however, we have another name for intercourse—"doing it"—and evidence shows that many don't much care whom they do it with.

Even a casual observer can tell you something has gone horribly wrong with sex in our time. But sex itself isn't the problem. God invented sex, after all, and He called it "very good" within His perfect creation. The problem with sex in our fallen world lies in the very nature of the plastic toyland we live in—and the plastic people playing around in that toyland.

The whirlwind of sexual immorality and depravity we're witnessing all around us is actually the death throes of a society that has lost its moorings, empty and adrift on a sea of loneliness. People keep on looking for reality but find only plastic. Seeking closeness and intimacy, people look everywhere—and so they find it nowhere. Wanting to be up close and personal, people try sex without commitment—and they end up even more alone and farther apart.

Once immorality meant a one-night stand or a visit to a prostitute. But we've come to new lows with the advent of "telephone sex," where disembodied voices exchange words and sounds calculated to excite and gratify without ever meeting one another. It's no longer sex without love; now it's sex with no intimacy at all. Is this what sex has come to in our anonymous world: long distance orgasm? You can call it sick, to be sure. But besides being sick, it is tragic. Horribly, sadly tragic. Could there be a more dismal commentary on the loneliness epidemic of our age?

The situation today is just as St. Paul described it 20 centuries ago:

> Although they claimed to be wise, they became fools. . . .
> Therefore God gave them over in the sinful desires of their hearts
> to sexual impurity for the degrading of their bodies with one
> another. . . . Although they know God's righteous decree that
> those who do such things deserve death, they not only continue
> to do these very things but also approve of those who practice
> them. (Rom. 1:22, 24, 32)

The sexual aberrations of our age are wrong and sinful, but
they're also extremely sad. This situation calls for something more
than outrage; it calls for genuine sorrow. Before we can ever clean
up our world we must weep for it. For what we see in today's sexual pollution is just another tragic symptom of the disease we all
share in this dying world—a disease called sin. Our sin of choice
may be different, but still we are all sinners. And *those who do such
things deserve death*. To paraphrase Pogo: "We have met the victims,
and they are us."

Some claim that sexual practices are becoming more guarded,
because of the AIDS epidemic. But the fact of faceless, empty sex
remains. And it's an ugly fact, for it shows us the emptiness of the
world we live in. Still more ugly is the fact that most of us refuse to
face facts. We continue to pretend that everything is just fine in this
world of ours.

The Big Lie

Most of the time the things I've talked about here are not problems for most of us. We manage to cope quite well with life; we've
actually convinced ourselves we're happy. We're content to go on
accumulating toys and demanding pleasure and calling it happiness.
We've grown accustomed to plastic things and plastic relationships;
we've even come to prefer them over the real thing. We don't mind
living behind barricades and in our private cubicles. We're perfectly
content to spend our lives walled off from other people. And we've
learned to live with surface talk and empty communication. We've
actually grown satisfied with loneliness—we call it drive and self-
sufficiency.

But as the century turns, maybe it's time we take another look
at the world we live in and evaluate it in the sober light of day.
Maybe it's time to quit fooling ourselves into believing that we are

"just fine" and that things are "just fine" and that everything will turn out "just fine."

The Naked Truth

Remember the old children's fable about the emperor's new clothes? An impostor had convinced everyone that he could weave magic clothes out of golden thread. To be sure, some noticed this thread was invisible. "Ah," said the tailor, "that's because only very wise people can see this cloth." Suddenly everyone pretended to see it, including the king, who ordered a full set of clothes made of the tailor's fictitious fabric. When the tailor pronounced his project finished, the king donned the make-believe wardrobe—and paraded down the street in his birthday suit! He was unwilling to admit he couldn't see the beautiful golden fabric. No one else was willing either. No one, that is, except for a small boy who had the audacity to say out loud what everyone already knew in their hearts: "The king isn't wearing anything at all!"

Who has the courage to take an honest look at this world of ours and call out the truth? Who has the heart to point out what we all know but are afraid to admit? Who will take a look at all this plastic and emptiness and loneliness and cheap imitation and describe what it really is? Who will call it?

God will call it. He calls it by one name. And it's a painfully simple name: death.

You and I can't go back to Eden. We live in a dying world. It's been in the process of dying ever since Adam and Eve elected themselves gods and thereby excluded themselves from the Tree of Life. We can deny it if we want. We can ignore it and try to escape it, but it won't work. For the truth is, you and I are dying too. Our laughter rings hollow in the playground we've tried to make of this world. And we've furnished this playground of ours with cheap imitation and ugly plastic.

The plain truth is, life isn't all we'd like it to be. Not only will we die one day; we are dying every day of our lives. We're dying to live, but we're dying just the same. Like it or not, that's the bottom line in the world we live in—everything else is pure sham. We're going to have to look somewhere else for real life.

25

The Surprising Alternative

Christianity is the unbelievably good news that there is forgiveness of sins, life, and salvation to be had in the midst of this dying world of ours. And this is the real thing; not just the same old rat race traded in for another treadmill. This is God's gift of life in exchange for death; LIFE in Person, in fact. In the person of Jesus Christ, who came *that they may have life, and have it to the full* (John 10:10).

And He is the one who shapes our life for the 21st century.

2

Our Living Lord

. . . in Christ all will be made alive. (1 Cor. 15:22)

Those early days of the tour had been exciting. The band drew plenty of media attention, and admiring crowds followed them everywhere they went. But then things changed. More and more hecklers interrupted their appearances. And the Leader himself just didn't seem the same any more. He talked increasingly about trouble and hardship—and even death.

Then one day he took the group aside. "I'm going away for a while," he told them. "But I'll come back and get you, because I want you guys with me wherever I am. And you know the way to the place I'm headed for."

Tom was confused. "We don't know where you're going," he protested. "So how can we know the way?"

"I am the way, and the truth, and the LIFE," said Jesus.

Life in Person

Death. There's no way around it. Despite our determined efforts to avoid it and cover it up, there's no escaping death. We can extend the human life span; we've even discovered some clues to the aging process, but ultimately every one of us comes face to face with death. All our lives are lived graveside. Dying to live, we're all dying just the same. That's the ugly reality.

But there is another reality just as real as death. More real, in fact: the reality of the life God brings into this dying world of ours.

People at the end of the 20th century aren't much interested in God. While there are some noticeable exceptions, our cultural mainstream isn't much in tune with the spiritual and the abstract. "What you see is what you get" is our basic approach to reality. And as I pointed out in the first chapter, what you see in the world today is pretty ugly.

And so at first hearing, all talk about God seems to be just talk; it doesn't seem to stand up to the hard realities of life in a dying world. No wonder, then, that a lot of people are turned off by Christianity. It sounds like religious double-talk. It looks like a crutch to escape reality. The very idea of eternal life in the midst of so much death seems out of place. It's whistling in the dark, a lot of people think; it was a nice idea, but that's just it—eternal life is simply an idea, nothing more.

But the life God brings into this world is not just an idea. God did not send an idea into the world, after all. He sent His Son. And Jesus Christ, God's Son, is life in person. *In him,* St. John writes, *was life, and that life was the light of men. . . . The Word became flesh and made his dwelling among us* (John 1:4, 14). This is not empty talk about life, this is life itself. In Jesus Christ, eternal life has made a personal appearance in this dying world of ours.

The Big Dilemma

God's personal appearance clashes with our view of reality. "What you see," we insist, "is what you get." And what we see isn't God or eternal life. We see hardship and struggle and loneliness. We see dying. We see death. God is supposed to bring life and light and joy, but we draw our conclusions based on what we see. God is intangible, untouchable, and therefore unreachable, we conclude.

Wise old King Solomon asked a very contemporary question: *Will God really dwell on earth?* He wondered whether God would actually take up residence in the stone and wood of the temple he constructed in Jerusalem. His answer was an astonished yes! (1 Kings 8:27 ff.)

Today we're wondering if God can be found in our world, too. But unlike Solomon, we don't know. Our answer is usually a skeptical shrug of the shoulders. We simply don't see the connection between the harsh realities around us and the whole idea of God. How can the physical contain the spiritual, we wonder. How can the natural embrace the supernatural? How is the finite capable of the infinite? Like oil and water, they simply don't mix, we assume.

Solomon found the infinite God within his finite temple. But modern man goes on looking, and wondering. Where in the world can we find God? Where can we find His life in the midst of our dying world? That's the big question as we approach the turn of the century.

The Shocking Answer

The disciples of Jesus were quite ordinary men, not all that different from common laborers today. Most of them were fishermen by trade. In the first century, as now, such men were not given to religious speculation or philosophical dreaming. They were rugged, down-to-earth men. Like us, they took their reality straight. And they measured reality by what could be seen and heard. But what they saw and heard in Jesus surprised them. John, one of the closest friends of Jesus, puts it this way:

> That which was from the beginning, which we have heard, which we have seen with our eyes, which we have looked at and our hands have touched—this we proclaim concerning the Word of life. The life appeared; we have seen it and testify to it, and we proclaim to you the eternal life, which was with the Father and has appeared to us. (1 John 1:1–2)

Never in the history of the world had such words been written. And never since has anyone claimed to find the infinite God within range of finite human senses. No one has ever claimed to touch God with human hands, or hear Him with human ears. It would have been a shock to King Solomon himself. After all, it's one thing to say the unseen God dwells within the quiet space of a beautiful sanctuary; it's quite another to maintain that He has taken up residence in tangible human flesh.

But this is the shocking claim of Jesus Christ.

God with Us

"Anyone has seen me," said Jesus, *"has seen the Father."* The religious leaders of Jesus' day couldn't tolerate this claim. They considered it sacrilege; to them it was an attack on the holiness of God. And we can understand why they felt that way. It was a preposterous claim to make. Buddha or Mohammed would never venture anywhere near that claim, since they thought of god as pure

29

spirit. Still today, thinking people find the whole idea of God clothed in human flesh too much to stomach. Everyone knows, after all, that the finite is not capable of the infinite. How can the all-powerful and the purely spiritual be contained within the confines of weak, physical human flesh? Solomon's question comes back in haunting refrain: *Will God really dwell on earth?*

No, insists human logic. Yes, says God. And God always has the last word.

The first man in the New Testament to be bowled over by God becoming flesh was Joseph. *A righteous man,* Matthew calls him (1:19). A fine, upstanding specimen of Jewish manhood. We can see from the text that he was not only a religious man, but also a sensible man, with his feet planted squarely in the real world. When Mary, his fianceé, was discovered to be pregnant, he knew he had no choice. Since he had not fathered this child, it was plain to him that Mary must have had sex with some other man; there could be no marriage.

And so Joseph quietly began breaking things off. But a messenger from God intervened. Reassuring him of Mary's virginity, the angel brought the astounding news that this child had no human father. This baby was one of a kind. He had been conceived by the power of the Holy Spirit. There was nothing, therefore, to interfere with Joseph's wedding plans. Matthew comments rather drily:

> All this took place to fulfill what the Lord had said through the prophet: "The virgin will be with child and will give birth to a son, and they will call him Immanuel"—which means, "God with us." (Matt. 1:22–23)

The impossible had happened. The infinite had taken on the finite. The spiritual was contained in the material. God had become man.

How can this be? That's our question. And it was Mary's, too, the first time she heard the news about her pregnancy.

> "How will this be," Mary asked the angel, "since I am a virgin?" The angel answered, "The Holy Spirit will come upon you, and the power of the Most High will overshadow you. So the holy one to be born will be called the Son of God. (Luke 1:34–35)

Will God really dwell on earth?—this was Solomon's big question. The answer came in a tiny package—a squirming infant boy:

Yes! God would dwell on earth. God does dwell on earth. The Father sends His Son to be conceived by His Spirit and born of a virgin mother.

Mary's baby is God in human flesh. And he has a name: *Immanuel:* GOD-WITH-US.

God and Man

Down through the centuries controversy has swirled around the person of Jesus. Not only the enemies of the church, but even teachers within the church had difficulty grasping how Jesus could possibly be both God and man at the same time. The oldest creeds, or summaries of Christian belief, were hammered out in lively debate over this pivotal paradox of the faith: the baby born in a barn at Bethlehem was in reality the almighty God clothed in human flesh.

"His only Son, our Lord," the Apostles' Creed says of Jesus. "True God from True God," is how the Nicene Creed describes his relationship to God the Father. "Perfect God and perfect man," the church confesses in the Athanasian Creed. This central mystery of the Incarnation, or the Son of God taking on human flesh, colors the entire Christian faith and life.

God in Diapers

The familiar Christmas narrative has become so entwined with pop culture that it has lost its original punch. As Luke tells it, the story is quite amazing. *"Today in the town of David a Savior has been born to you; he is Christ the Lord,"* the heavenly messenger announced to the shepherds. The word *Christ* (literally "Anointed One") was familiar to them; it was the Old Testament title for the Messiah, the deliverer promised to Israel. Through the centuries their ancestors had been looking for just such a Christ to be born. But when the angel called this newborn Christ "the Lord" it must have sent shivers up the shepherds' spines.

"Lord" (*Kyrios*) was a pseudonym for the name God himself had revealed to his people: YHWH. Out of respect for God, Israel never uttered His sacred name aloud; Israel always substituted "Lord." The

31

angel was telling the astonished shepherds that the long-awaited Christ was actually God Himself.

This Christ was God, in other words. Amazing enough. But what must have really astounded the shepherds is that they would find the Holy One of Israel in such a small package. *"This will be a sign to you,"* the angel announced. *"You will find a baby wrapped in cloths and lying in a manger."* They were to look for an ordinary baby in an extraordinary place. You don't expect to find infants in cattle troughs, after all. The manger was an extraordinary cradle for this baby. But it was an ordinary baby, that's for sure. *"Wrapped in cloths,"* He was. And for good reason. Babies in those days were always wrapped in cloths—just as we diaper our newborns today.

Solomon's age-old question was answered at Bethlehem, and with an exclamation point. Yes, God would really dwell on earth with man! This baby born to a young Jewish virgin was God with us. God couldn't get more "with us" than He did in Jesus. God couldn't dwell more completely on earth than He did in Jesus. He not only shares our humanity, he shares our very skin and bones. He's really one of us. He not only shares our human flesh, he came in infant flesh, wrapped in diapers and cradled in a manger.

Luke records that when Mary heard what the angels told the shepherds about her child, she *treasured up all these things and pondered them in her heart.* There's not much more you can really do with such information, is there? The Incarnation hits people that way. When it dawns on you that the infant Jesus is actually God in diapers, cold analysis won't do; the heart is activated. Speculation changes into reflection. Doubt gives way to faith. Intellectual appraisal comes to a halt. Prayer takes over.

Antidote to Death

There in the manger was the answer to the dilemma of mankind. God Himself lay helpless in the hay: the deepest mystery and most profound reality that ever occurred in this world of ours. *In Christ,* writes St. Paul, *all the fullness of the Deity lives in bodily form* (Col. 2:9). The immortal God lay clothed in mortal flesh. And in this infant boy, Life itself had come to taste of death.

People keep thinking that Christianity is a highly complex system for moral reform, a kind of self-improvement program launched by Jesus. Certainly there are moral implications in the Christian gospel, but it's definitely not a self-improvement program. In fact, it's not even a way of life—as you and I would normally think of it. Christianity is instead Life itself: the Life Jesus Christ gives us to live.

This is the testimony, St. John said: *God has given us eternal life, and this life is in his Son* (1 John 5:11). This statement stands out more boldly when we remember the basic human predicament is not the moral mess we live in but rather the death that lives in us. Sure, we're all caught in the tangled web of sin and its effects on our lives, but all these ugly actions find their origin in something uglier still: our own sinful heart. This is the real dilemma—not the rotten situation we live in, but the rottenness living in us.

As I made clear in the first chapter, it's not a simple cosmetic problem. The stench of death filters from our very pores.

But now Life has entered this dying world. Life in person. Life in Jesus Christ. In His very flesh all the fullness of God lived in bodily form. And that flesh of His was not only the perfect offering for sin. It was the antidote to death; the source of Life for the world.

In the sixth chapter of John's gospel, Jesus speaks about Himself as death's antidote:

> "I tell you the truth, he who believes has everlasting life. I am the bread of life. Your forefathers ate the manna in the desert, yet they died. But here is the bread that comes down from heaven, which a man may eat and not die. I am the living bread that came down from heaven. If anyone eats of this bread, he will live forever. This bread is my flesh, which I will give for the life of the world." (John 6:47–51)

While the Israelites were fed miraculously in their wilderness wanderings by manna from heaven, that food was for the body only. Ultimately, the people fed with this heavenly bread still died.

There is another kind of bread from heaven, however. This bread is food for body and soul. It is the source of heavenly Life; those who eat of this bread share in a life that transcends the grave. *"This bread,"* Jesus dramatically asserts, *"is my flesh which I will give for the life of the world."*

The Hidden God

"What you see is what you get," human logic insists. Jesus shows us differently. In His physical body was much more than could be seen with the naked eye. Hiding under the humanity of Jesus, God Himself had come to take up residence in this world. Now that seems strange to us; why should God want to hide Himself? If Jesus is truly God, why wouldn't that be immediately obvious to everyone? Why this hide-and-seek game?

But God doesn't play games with people. It's not that He wants to hide from anyone. In fact, He wants to make Himself known to everyone. It's just that to reveal Himself, He has to hide. If He didn't, we'd all be dead meat.

That's how Isaiah saw himself: dead meat. He caught a glimpse of God in a vision during the temple liturgy, and he was flabbergasted. *"Woe to me,"* he cried, *"I am ruined For I am a man of unclean lips, and I live among a people of unclean lips, and my eyes have seen the King, the LORD Almighty"* (Is. 6:5). How could he—polluted by sin as he was—enter the holy presence of God without being consumed? The Lord took away Isaiah's sin and commissioned him to speak His Word. Without God's cleansing word of forgiveness, Isaiah would have been dead meat in His presence.

None of us would dare touch a power line deliberately. The sheer power of the energy could kill us. In fact, electrical current must be transformed to lower its intensity before it comes into our homes, or it would burn out even our appliances.

God is definitely interested in making Himself known to us. But He certainly doesn't want to destroy anyone in the process. That's why He hides. It seems like a contradiction, but it's absolutely true. In order to contact us, God hides Himself.

The Back Side of God

Moses was like us. He believed what you see is what you get. Yet Moses never saw God. Moses heard from God, but He never saw God with his eyes. And Moses, like us, got tired of living by faith. He wanted to live by sight. *"Now show me your glory,* he called out in frustration" (Ex. 33:18).

"I will proclaim my name, the LORD in your presence. . . . But
. . . you cannot see my face, for no one may see me and live. . . .
There is a place near me where you may stand on a rock. When
my glory passes by, I will put you in a cleft in the rock and cover
you with my hand until I have passed by. Then I will remove my
hand and you will see my back; but my face must not be seen"
(Ex. 33:19–23)

What God did for Moses centuries before, He was doing for all
mankind at Bethlehem. There all the fullness of God was hiding
under the humanity of the infant Jesus. He, the hope of all the
world, was laid in a cattle trough. God in diapers. Though He feeds
the birds of the air and the fish of the sea, He nursed at His mother's
breast like any other newborn. It boggles the mind.

Mary *treasured up all these things and pondered them in her
heart,* Luke informs us (2:19). "It needs to be pondered in the
heart," Luther once wrote, "what it means to be the mother of God."
God was hiding there in the tiny infant she held in her arms. But He
didn't want to hide from us. He hid in flesh in order to bring Life
into this dying world of ours.

Despite popular artistic depictions of the birth of Jesus, there
were no halos that night. Anyone who looked in upon the manger
would have seen nothing more than a newborn boy lying in the
hay. "What you see is what you get," insists human logic. Faith
replies: "Hush; there's more here than meets the eye. When you
look at this baby, you're looking at God: the back side of God."

And so in Jesus Life came to this dying world to taste of death.

The Medicine of Immortality

In Jesus Christ, God walked the earth in human flesh. That body
of His was the antidote to the death of humanity. Crucified, risen,
and ascended in glory, His human flesh is still the remedy for the
death of man, for it contains the Life of God. Enclosed within His
physical flesh, God's deathless power entered this terminally ill
world. And today Jesus Christ remains the medicine of Life for our
death.

Every other man who ever walked the face of the earth even-
tually ended up as a permanent victim of death—except this man,
Jesus. He is the victor over death. *It was impossible for death to*

keep its hold on him, said Peter (Acts 2:24). For He is life, life personified. *In Him,* St. John bluntly asserts, *was life, and that life was the light of men* (John 1:4). This man is different from all other men. This man is God. And He is God for us.

A Great Mystery

"Who for us men and for our salvation came down from heaven and was Incarnate by the Holy Spirit of the virgin Mary and was made man." That's the way Christians have confessed the incarnation down through the centuries in the Nicene Creed. God took on human flesh for us. Jesus Christ is both true God, begotten of the Father from eternity, and also true man, born of His virgin mother. Therefore in the human flesh of Jesus, God was laid in a manger for us. God was wrapped in cloths for us. God in diapers—for us. God on a cross—for us. God dead—for us. This is the heart of the matter; in Jesus Christ, God Himself submitted to death in order to give us life. When this glorious truth breaks in, human wisdom grinds to a halt. Faith takes over. Knees bend in adoration and mouths open to stammer out His praise.

No wonder the authors of the New Testament spoke in hushed tones about the whole astounding wonder: *mysterion,* they called it—mystery.

> Beyond all question, the mystery of godliness is great: He appeared in a body, was vindicated by the Spirit, was seen by angels, was preached among the nations, was believed on in the world, was taken up in glory. (1 Tim. 3:16)

But the mystery intensifies. Notice I have spoken of Jesus in the present tense. He is true God for us. Not only was He God, but He is God. Not only was He God for us, but He is God for us. This mystery is not locked up in history or separated from our world today by the chasm of time. This mystery of God made flesh for the salvation of mankind is a present reality for His church. The same God who appeared on earth in a body and was taken up into heaven is present with His church wherever His Word is preached and His Sacraments distributed.

This, too, is a mystery. Not a "who done it?" kind of mystery, but the mystery the New Testament writers had in mind as they described the God who came to earth in His Son, Jesus Christ. In Him was life. His physical flesh was embodied life, which Jesus gave into death for the life of the world. His body was the stuff of heaven come down to earth. When you heard Jesus, you heard God. When you saw Jesus, you saw God. When you touched Jesus, you touched God. This is the mystery—that all the fullness of God Himself was hidden in the physical body of Jesus. He is, in fact, a tangible earthly link with eternity.

But not many people ever heard, saw, or touched Jesus. What about the rest of us? No problem, the New Testament informs us. Time and space are no barrier:

> That which was from the beginning, which we have heard, which we have seen with our eyes, which we have looked at and our hands have touched—this we proclaim concerning the Word of life. The life appeared; we have seen it and testify to it, and we proclaim to you the eternal life, which was with the Father and has appeared to us. (1 John 1:1–2)

The Mysteries of God

This is how one should regard us, wrote the apostle Paul of himself and his fellow pastors, *as servants of Christ and stewards of the mysteries of God* (1 Cor. 4:1 RSV). Paul was no opportunist. He wasn't trying to call attention to himself. Rather, he was pointing to God's ongoing action through His Son. Through Jesus Christ, God the Father continues to dispense His deathless Life in our dying world by the power of His Spirit. And He uses earthly channels to do it. Just as Christ Himself is the mystery of God—our earthly link with heaven—so also those earthly activities He has given to the church are to be regarded as mysteries—tangible links with eternity.

"The words I have spoken to you," said Jesus, *"are spirit and they are life"* (John 6:63). His words extend and apply all that was embodied in Him and accomplished by Him. Just as Christ Himself is our life, so His words are life. And He commissioned His servants to speak His word. *"He who listens to you listens to me,"* He said (Luke 10:16). In the proclamation of His Gospel, the Lord of life still speaks through human mouthpieces in His church throughout time.

Faith comes from hearing the message (Rom. 10:17), wrote St. Paul. It's no small wonder that human words could serve as a vehicle of spiritual power. But then, these are no ordinary words. These are the words of Christ. They are earthly links with heaven. The words of His gospel breathe life into our dying world. It is the life of Christ, who is our life. *"I am the Living One,"* He calls to His church from His seat in glory. *"I was dead, and behold I am alive for ever and ever"* (Rev. 1:18). The word of Christ is one of the mysteries He has given His church.

But there are others. Particularly that washing we know as Holy Baptism and that meal we know as the Holy Supper, or Communion. These too are the mysteries of God—Holy Sacraments which God has given His church on earth in order to bring us life. The very word *sacrament,* in fact, comes from the Latin word for "mystery."

Water and Blood

Immediately our human intellect objects: How can water have any spiritual effect? How can eating and drinking provide spiritual benefits? What you see is what you get, we're inclined to insist.

But the Lord of life continues to operate in our world today just as he has always done—in hidden ways. Still today we gaze upon the back side of God in water, bread, and wine. The mighty power of His Word is still hidden in lowly external coverings. The same God who came wrapped in physical flesh in the stable at Bethlehem still reaches into our life by way of tangible earthly matter. Through these Sacraments, Jesus Christ dispenses today all the benefits of His saving work accomplished long ago.

Two pivotal events mark the public career of Jesus. He launched His rescue mission at the River Jordan, where He was baptized, and He finished His work some three years later at Calvary where He was crucified. Like bookends, these two events enclose the entire saving work of God-in-flesh.

These two events—the baptism of Jesus and His death on the cross—contain between them the work of God in exchanging His Life for the life of the world: Jordan and Calvary. River and cross. Water and blood.

> This is the one who came by water and blood—Jesus Christ. He did not come by water only, but by water and blood. And it is the Spirit who testifies, because the Spirit is the truth. For there are three that testify: the Spirit, the water and the blood; and the three are in agreement. (1 John 5:6–8)

In this passage, John links the saving work of Jesus to the Sacraments of the church. As there was a past reality, so there is a present reality. Jesus not only came by water and by blood, but there are three that testify: the Spirit, the water, and the blood. In other words, the Holy Spirit continues in every age to breathe life into this dying world by bringing the work of the Lord of life to bear upon His church. The one who came by water and by blood still comes hidden in water and blood: the water of Baptism and the blood of the Holy Supper.

More about that later. For now, note this remarkable scene at the cross recorded by the same disciple, John. The soldiers were under orders to hasten the death of the crucifixion victims so their bodies could be taken down before the Sabbath began.

> But when they came to Jesus and found that he was already dead, they did not break his legs. Instead, one of the soldiers pierced Jesus' side with a spear, bringing a sudden flow of blood and water. (John 19:33–34)

Just a coincidence? Hardly. Jesus Christ, who stepped into death in the water of the Jordan and who conquered death by the blood of Calvary, feeds and nourishes the church sacramentally in every age by water and by blood. In the very face of death and by means of His death, the Lord of life has purchased life for our dying world. There is hope for the likes of us.

"You are my Son, whom I love; in You I am well pleased," said the Father when Jesus stood in the Jordan, wet with the water of His baptism (Luke 3:22). *"Father, into your hands I commit my spirit,"* said Jesus in His bleeding death on the cross (23:46). Here we see that death has lost its terror. The Father loved the world so much that He gave His only begotten Son into our death that we might live. As Jesus Christ was well pleasing to the Father in His baptism, so He was well pleasing in His death. The sacramental washing and meal of Jesus enfold us in the death of Jesus. In His death, there

is life. And so history repeats itself once more. In Jesus Christ, you and I are also well pleasing to our Father in heaven.

There is more to the Sacraments than what first appears. You get much more than you can see; a hidden reality stands behind them. The water of Holy Baptism and the body and blood of the Holy Supper find their source in the very body of Him in whom all the fullness of the godhead dwells bodily. From His side at Calvary gushed forth water and blood for His church in every age of this dying world.

And there is life in that blood. It is the very life of God.

3

Our Death/His Cross

He humbled himself and became obedient to death—even death on a cross! (Phil. 2:8)

"No, I'd really rather not." His voice was firm, though weary.

"But think again," his companion insisted. "You can have it all. Fortune, fame, and power. It's all mine to give, and I dish it out at will. I make and break the best of men. I can set you up for good. Let me have it my way just this once—you'll see."

"Begone, Satan," said Jesus.

Our Great Hero

The stage was set for conflict. In tiny infant flesh the Lord of life came to taste of death. Yet He is Lord of all. *"No one takes [my life] from me,"* He said. *"I lay it down of my own accord"* (John 10:18). No need to feel sorry for Jesus. He was no helpless pawn in the hands of the power brokers of this world. He was no supporting actor in the continuing saga of man's inhumanity to man. The stakes were much higher. This was a cosmic battle, and Jesus came out on top. It was a fight to the death, and Jesus won the victory by His death. For once, the victim emerged the victor. The cross is not tragedy, but triumph. It is the crowning achievement of Jesus, the Epiphany King.

Visitors from the East

Those of us with fond memories of Christmas pageants might be a bit disappointed in Matthew's account of the birth of Jesus. After all, he omits some of the best scenes from the more familiar narrative in Luke's gospel. No angel choruses, no hurried shepherds rushing off to Bethlehem, no quaint manger scene. Matthew's gospel leaps right over all that. The scene shifts from Joseph's mar-

41

riage to a pregnant virgin directly to the arrival of the Magi after Mary's child was born:

> When Joseph woke up, he did what the angel of the Lord had commanded him and took Mary home as his wife. But he had no union with her until she gave birth to a son. And he gave him the name Jesus. After Jesus was born in Bethlehem in Judea, during the time of King Herod, Magi from the east came to Jerusalem. (Matt. 1:24–25, 2:1)

Since these men came from eastern territory, the church has called their visit to the child Jesus the *epiphany*, or "manifestation." It revealed that the Father's love is unsegregated; Jesus came not just for God's chosen people, Israel, but for all mankind. And so these exotic visitors in Matthew's gospel give hope to us all.

Just exactly who these men were, we don't know. Astrologers, some would have it. Professional stargazers. Religious gurus. Tradition, building on the royal gifts they presented to the child in Bethlehem, calls them "the three kings." There's nothing in the record, however, limiting their number to three. And almost certainly they were not kings. The point is, we know little about these men. They appear, as it were, out of nowhere. But the stated purpose of their journey was extremely upsetting to the King of Judea, and it threw the whole city into a commotion.

> "Where is the one who has been born king of the Jews? We saw his star in the east and have come to worship him." When King Herod heard this he was disturbed, and all Jerusalem with him. (Matt. 2:2–3)

Herod was just the kind of monarch who would be threatened by such news. A paranoid, power-hungry ruler, history tells us he arranged the assassinations of several of his own sons in order to protect his throne. And so Herod hatched a plot to dispatch the threat of this infant king as well. He solicited the Magi's help: *He sent them to Bethlehem and said, "Go and make a careful search for the child. As soon as you find him, report to me, so that I too may go and worship him"* (Matt. 2:8). It sounded like a pious request, but he was lying through his teeth. Herod had no serious plans for worship; the slaughter he arranged later for all infant boys in Bethlehem betrayed his real intent (2:16). But God intervened, and Jesus' life was spared—for the time being.

His Manifest Destiny

Thus the cross cast its shadow over the Lord of life already in His infancy. For this murderous episode was a shadow of things to come for Jesus. Death loomed ahead. It was actually His job description, you might say. True God and true man at the same time, Jesus Christ was intent on a rescue operation by which He sealed His own destiny.

> Since the children have flesh and blood, he too shared in their humanity so that by his death he might destroy him who holds the power of death—that is, the devil—and free those who all their lives were held in slavery by their fear of death. (Heb. 2:14–15)

A death sentence hung over all humanity, and the death of God was the only way out from under that sentence. Mankind was in bondage, death's hostage. And so death had to die. But life itself was the price—the life of God embodied in the human flesh of Jesus. There was no way around death for Jesus. He came, He insisted, for this very purpose: *"to give his life as a ransom for many"* (Mark 10:45).

The Magi were right when they called Jesus a king, but in a way they never imagined. The tiny baby born in Bethlehem was indeed a king. But this king was different. His kingdom, He informed Pilate years later, was not of this world. And sure enough, He didn't operate like an earthly king. True to form, the God who hid in human flesh to save us hid His royal majesty under shame and dishonor. His power was manifest in weakness, His glory in disgrace. His crown was made of thorns, and His throne a wooden cross. As victim He won our victory. In defeat He achieved the conquest. Death was His destiny. And the cross was His destination.

But this glorious saga began long before He was nailed up to die.

The Jordan Connection

It all started at the Jordan. There the eccentric prophet John had set up his center of operations, *preaching a baptism of repentance for the forgiveness of sins,* St. Mark records (1:4). Clothed in camel hair and leather, eating locusts and wild honey, John ("the Baptizer," he is commonly labeled) was the very picture of the famous prophet Elijah, who had called Israel to repentance in the days of King Ahab. The people of Judea and Jerusalem flocked out into the Jordanian wilderness to hear him. They believed he was the forerunner of the promised deliverer, as Malachi had foretold: *See, I will send you the prophet Elijah before that great and dreadful day of the LORD comes* (4:5).

John identified himself as the "voice calling in the desert." Centuries before, Isaiah had predicted such a messenger would appear to "prepare the way for the Lord" (40:3). And so there in the desert along the Jordan River John set up camp, preaching his fiery message of repentance in anticipation of the Lord's coming:

> "The ax is already at the root of the trees, and every tree that does not produce good fruit will be cut down and thrown into the fire. I baptize you with water for repentance. But after me will come one who is more powerful than I, whose sandals I am not fit to carry. He will baptize you with the Holy Spirit and with fire." (Matt. 3:10–11)

Confessing their sins, [people] were baptized by [John], Matthew records (3:6). So when Jesus stepped up for baptism, John objected. *I need to be baptized by you,* he said (3:14). And we know what John meant. After all, since Jesus had no sins of His own to confess, how could He qualify for John's baptism? Never mind, replied Jesus. He insisted that He be baptized anyway. *"It is proper for us to do this to fulfill all righteousness,"* He responded (3:15). He wanted to take on our sin, you see. He insisted on bearing our guilt. For He was intent on dying our death.

And die He did. Ultimately, He breathed His last after hours of excruciating shame on a cross. *He was pierced for our transgressions,* Isaiah prophesied (53:5), *He was crushed for our iniquities.* It was a borrowed death Jesus died, in other words. It was our death. But it brought life to us. *By His wounds,* Isaiah explains, *we are healed.*

And His baptism was not his own. It was ours. By His baptism in the Jordan Jesus took upon Himself the obligation of the sins of the world. There He took up His cross as realistically as when Pilate's soldiers laid a crossbeam on His shoulders. At the Jordan the sinless Son of God was made to be sin for us. The die was cast. His destination was sealed in the water of His baptism. At the Jordan, the Lord of life stepped heroically into death. For since the wages of sin is death, the baptism of Jesus pointed relentlessly to His cross and death.

The Tempter's Ploy

Given a choice, no human being deliberately chooses the cross. No one picks weakness, suffering, and affliction over strength, power, and prestige. You and I prefer the path of glory rather than the path of the cross. It's been that way ever since our first parents caved in to the temptation of the devil.

The devil is a case of rebellion gone berserk. The Bible informs us that the devil is a rebel angel, the sinister source of all evil in the world. Not content with his position as one of God's angelic servants, he aspired to be like God. The Scriptures variously describe the devil as the tempter and the destroyer, but he's perhaps best known by his most descriptive name: Satan, which means "accuser." He takes perverse delight in accusing God's children, pointing out their guilt and shame.

An Ancient Drama

In Adam all die, the Apostle reminds us (1 Cor. 15:22). And that's the tragic consequence of the famous temptation in the Garden of Eden. On the surface it was a simple act: eating the forbidden fruit. But on a deeper level, a lot more was at stake. Adam and his wife fell for the devil's favorite tactic. They chose their own prestige over the word of God. *"You must not eat from the tree of the knowledge of good and evil,"* the Creator had told them, *"for when you eat of it you will surely die"* (Gen. 2:17). *"You will not surely die,"* the devil blatantly argued. *"For God knows that when you eat of it your eyes will be opened, and you will be like God, knowing good and evil"* (3:5).

It was a half-truth. Before they had known only good, and now they would know evil as well. That much was true. But when you aspire to be like God you lose something. You lose life. You end up with death. That's what happened to Adam and Eve and to every single human being since Adam fell for the devil's deceit.

"A liar and the father of lies," Jesus called him (John 8:44). And He should know, from personal experience. For Jesus also went head to head with the devil. In Eden the tempter conquered Adam. But in the Jordan desert the tables were turned. It was a new scene, but the same drama. And the temptation of Jesus in the desert ushered in the final act. At Calvary Jesus Christ won victory over the devil. But that victory began in the Jordan desert. There a new Adam gained the upper hand. Jesus Christ, God in human flesh, stood toe to toe with the devil. But this time the devil lost.

A New Actor

Satan didn't pull any punches; he threw every trick in the book at Jesus. Hunger, power, prestige—all became weapons in the devil's arsenal. The devil tried every way he could to get Jesus to avoid the cross. You will be like God, he had gloated to Eve and her husband. *"All this I will give you,"* he promised Jesus, *"if you will bow down and worship me"* (Matt. 4:9). Here at the Jordan a new actor played in Eden's drama. Once again a perfect man confronted sin. And once again the life of mankind hung in the balance.

Fresh from the water of His baptism, Jesus was headed for the cross. Now the devil called that destination into question. His whole mission was up for grabs. Would Jesus be victimized by Satan? Would He fall for the lie that glory is better than the cross? Would He pick prestige over suffering, power over weakness, life over death?

The answer came in no uncertain terms. Our great Epiphany King stood His ground. Jesus Christ, the Lord of all life, met every temptation of the evil one head on with the sure word of God. Ultimately, he told the devil to go to hell: *"Away from me, Satan! For it is written: 'Worship the Lord your God, and serve him only' "* (Matt. 4:10). Jesus would not be deterred from the cross. For the wages of our sin is death. And Jesus came into this dying world determined to pay our debt. Nothing would distract Him; He came, He said, *"to give his life as a ransom for many"* (Mark 10:45). From the beginning in Jordan to the end at Calvary he had only one resolute purpose.

And so there's a link between Jordan and Calvary, between water and blood, between river and cross. That link is death—the death of God for the life of the world.

The Offense of the Cross

Somehow the cross has lost its punch for the majority of us. When so many crosses hang on so many of our walls and adorn so many of our sanctuaries, St. Paul's dramatic claim seems strange: *the message of the cross is foolishness to those who are perishing* (1 Cor. 1:18). Having been a standard form of costume jewelry and a routine piece in punk rock regalia, the cross has lost some of its shock value. Yet even our jaded ears can hear a certain bite in the Apostle's blunt words. The preaching of the cross, he insists, is *a stumbling block to Jews and foolishness to Gentiles* (1:23).

And the cross is offensive to the human mind, once you grasp its underlying message. On the surface, the cross seems quite tame. Moviegoers have gotten used to blood and gore as standard fare. But there's nothing entertaining about the cross. Though there was plenty of blood and gore at Calvary, the message of the cross goes much deeper. There was much more there than met the eye. It was not just a question of the torture Jesus endured, but the shame He bore.

The Shame of the Cross

Curiosity seekers saw nothing unique at Calvary. For them the cross of Jesus was nothing new. They had seen it all before. There was a sordid routine to every execution under Roman rule: first the stripping, then the flogging, finally the nailing. In the end every crucifixion looked much the same. Jagged, bleeding human flesh was nailed up to die a horrible death. For some victims it meant weeks of agony before they finally died of exposure and suffocation, no longer able to muster enough strength to fill their aching lungs.

On the surface it was the same for Jesus as it had been for all the others. Stripped of His clothing, He was nailed up to die a naked, shameful death, the butt of jokes by a mob of jeering bystanders. The governor's official indictment hung over His head in bitter mockery: *Jesus of Nazareth, the King of the Jews* (John 19:19).

He didn't look like a king. In fact, with that poster overhead, He looked like a pitiful clown. The jeering mob thought they had the last laugh: *"He saved others,"* they shouted, *"but he can't save himself."* But He didn't come to save Himself. He came to save us. This was His determined purpose: to give His life for the life of the world. *For the joy set before him,* the Apostle reminds us, He *endured the cross, scorning its shame* (Heb. 12:2). Gladly He laid down His life. Willingly He bore our sin. Joyfully He embraced our shame. And that is the heart of the matter.

There's guilt connected with sin, it's true. But shame is the real killer. "Guilt" is abstract, after all. We shrug it off all too easily. Just as Adam blamed Eve for his sin, we can pass our guilt on to others. But there's no passing off shame. It lies there, deep inside the human heart; an ugly, festering wound within.

There's a biting pain to shame. It might be remorse for injury we've caused others or humiliation because of injuries we've received. Humiliation, remorse, disgrace—it's all the same. It all adds up to one great big ugly painful wound called shame. And it won't be ignored. Shame can be removed, but it cannot be ignored.

Jesus did not ignore our shame. He removed it. Though He was God, He *made himself nothing, taking the very nature of a servant, being made in human likeness. And being found in appearance as a man, he humbled himself and became obedient to death—even death on a cross* (Phil. 2:7–8). In His naked, shameful death at the cross, the Lord of life embraced not merely sin's guilt, but its shame as well. He bore the biting pain of our shame in His very body, *and by his wounds we are healed* (Is. 53:5).

It was an ugly scene that day at Calvary. But more was there than met the eye. Pilate's biting parody proclaimed ironic truth. *The King of the Jews,* he had inscribed above this naked, dying man. And Jesus was in fact a king, though He governed no real estate and commanded no earthly armies. The mysterious Magi first introduced God's awesome saga, and here was its final chapter. The promised king had come, but His kingdom was not of this world. He, God in human flesh, had come to die. The cosmic king laid down His life for the life of the world.

The Death of God

This is the true offense of the cross—that God died for the sins of the world. True, there is life in the cross for us all, but that life begins with the death of Jesus. And Jesus is God. All the fullness of God was confined within His flesh. When Jesus died, God died. It's as simple as that and as profoundly mind-boggling as that. All complex theological argument and intellectual debate recede in the face of the cross. You don't argue your way to this truth. You don't arrive at this conclusion by rational debate. Human wisdom will always consider this message foolishness and weakness. *But the foolishness of God is wiser than man's wisdom, and the weakness of God is stronger than man's strength* (1 Cor. 1:25) .

And so this foolish, weak cross of Jesus is the heart and center of the Christian faith. All other reality flows from it. In this dying world we have no other hope beside the cross of Christ and its message—the death of God for the life of the world.

The Agony of Defeat

When it was all over that day at Calvary, they took His body down and placed it in a tomb. "Was crucified, died, and was buried," the church confesses in her ancient baptismal creed. This triad belongs together, like three hammer blows nailing down for all time the reality of what happened at the cross. This was no picture or symbol of the love of God for mankind. Here was love in concrete, stark reality: God in flesh laid low in death, buried in a grave. It was a real grave, for it was a real death.

And it looked like defeat. Even to his own disciples, the death of Jesus looked like defeat. Luke records the despair of two disciples from Emmaus. Walking home in the aftermath of Calvary, they conversed with a stranger, who seemed blissfully ignorant of the whole sordid affair. They filled him in on the tragic events of the week just gone by. Jesus of Nazareth, they explained, the one on whom they had pinned their hopes, was no more. *The chief priests and our rulers handed him over to be sentenced to death, and they crucified him; we had hoped that he was the one who was going to redeem Israel* (Luke 24:20–21). Couched in the past tense, their words dripped with bitter disappointment. We had hoped. Once there was hope, but now no more. All hope for the redemption of Israel was dead and gone, buried with their crucified Lord.

"Was crucified, died and was buried": that's the way it happened, and that's the way they laid it out for the stranger who seemed to be so blind about Jesus. Couldn't he see the futility of it all? But they were the ones who couldn't see. The man who walked with them was none other than Jesus Christ Himself, risen from the grave. Later their eyes would be opened to recognize Him, when He broke bread and gave it to them. But even in their blindness His words burned with joy for despairing hearts. *"Did not the Christ have to suffer these things and then enter his glory?"* He asked. Unfolding the Scriptures to them, he explained how God's plan for victory included defeat on the cross from the very beginning.

The Thrilling Victory

From the day of Adam's rebellion, this life-filled world has always been on the brink of death. And it's no different for us. Dying to live, we're dying just the same. But in the midst of death there is life. It is the life of Jesus Christ, whose very flesh embodies life. Handing over that life into death He won life for us all. Giving His body and shedding His blood, the Lord of life gave Himself for the life of the world.

In His death on His cross, this living Lord brought life to our dying world. And Christ's death on His cross also means the death of death itself. It was predicted centuries before it happened. *On this mountain,* Isaiah prophesied, *the LORD almighty. . . . will destroy the shroud that enfolds all peoples, the sheet that covers all nations; he will swallow up death forever. [He] . . . will wipe away the tears from all faces; he will remove the disgrace of his people from all the earth. The LORD has spoken* (Is. 25:6–8).

All of that came true at Calvary. "Golgotha," they called that site "the Place of the Skull." It was a place of death, and the cross was the tool of death. But in that very place and with that very tool God shattered our shackles of bondage and defeated our dread enemy. At Calvary the Lord of life on His cross snatched victory from the jaws of defeat. *"It is finished,"* Jesus called out with his dying breath (John 19:30). And it was. When He died, all the power of sin and death died with Him. In His death Jesus Christ swallowed up death forever. The death of Christ meant the death of death. That's why the cross brings life. It is the life of Christ, which is always life from out of death.

There is life for our dying world. It is life in connection with Jesus: risen for us all, but first "crucified, died, and buried." There was no road to life for Him except through death. And it's the same for us. There's no way around death. You can either die alone in this world or you can die in Jesus. You can have life your way or you can have it His way. Your way leads through life to death. His way leads through death into life.

The Baptism Connection

There is no road to life in this world apart from Jesus. But we need not live apart from Him. He has given His church in every age a genuine link with His saving work. That link is Baptism. Baptism is a link with both Jordan and Calvary, with the river where He first confronted our death and with the cross where He ultimately triumphed by His own death. The road of Jesus Christ always leads through death into life. Sharing in His death by our baptism, we also share in His resurrection, the Apostle explains: *Christ being raised from the dead will never die again; death no longer has dominion over him* (Rom. 6:9 RSV). Thus Baptism into Christ is the real key to life.

From His life-giving body flowed water in his death. And the link between our dying world and the living Lord is the washing He has given His church. It is a life-giving water, for it is our link with the crucified and risen Lord. *As many of you as were baptized into Christ have put on Christ,* the Apostle wrote (Gal. 3:27 NKJV). In the midst of our dying world every baptized child of God has a share in never-ending life. By Baptism we die in Christ; by Baptism we live in Christ.

There's life in that death of His. And so there is life in His washing. It is the very life of God.

PART 2

The Sacramental Focus of the Christian Life

4

Holy Baptism: Water of Life

Baptism . . . now saves you. (1 Peter 3:21)

Peter Johnson was dumbfounded. It just didn't seem right. Bad enough no waiter was available at the biggest corporate dinner of the year. But what had gotten into the boss? Here he was, making his way around the table, serving each man one by one. And they just sat there and let him continue! When the boss came to him, Pete intervened. "I'm sorry, sir," he said, "But I can't accept this. Why would you want to serve me?"

Jesus looked up quizzically, his hands still wet from the basin. His words were kind and inviting: "If I don't wash you, you have no part in me."

Through Death to Life

Dying to live. It sounds strange, but that's exactly how Christ brings life into this dying world. Through death; His death on the cross. From His body flowed blood and water that day, the signs of His death. But they are signs of life for us. In fact, there's no other way to live than through the death of Jesus. We're all dying; we can either die alone, or we can die in Jesus. But His death brings life, and it's when we die with Him that we really begin to live.

The Great Paradox

I've already shown how God does things backwards in Jesus Christ. That is, He always seems to act exactly opposite from what you and I would expect. He shows His power in weakness, His glory in shame, His majesty in lowliness. From the day the angel announced to Mary that the embryo within her was none other than the Son of God until that day the soldiers took His body down from the cross and some friends buried Him in a borrowed grave, there

55

was always more to Jesus than met the eye. What you see is what you get, we think. But that's not the way it is with Jesus. When you looked at Jesus, you were actually looking at the back side of God.

But the back side of God and His backwards ways were not an attempt to hide from us. He was actually hiding—in seeming weakness and apparent foolishness—so He could reveal Himself all the more clearly. God backed into our world, so to speak, in order that we could face Him without being annihilated in our sin. It was His way of being up front and personal.

And the cross is about as personal as God can get. In Eden, Adam and Eve hid their shame from God. At Calvary a new Adam was clothed in naked human shame. But He didn't hide. The Lord of life did not hide from either God or man. On His cross He openly displayed His love for all to see. It was a hidden love, wrapped up in shame and death so that we might have His intimate love and life here in this dying world of ours.

And out of the body of Jesus flowed water in His death. It was water drenched in life; the life of God for the death of mankind. But that water flowed out from death: the death of God for the life of the world. Nothing else would do.

The Destroyer Destroyed

If the children of Adam were to go on living, then death had to die. And there was only one way death could die; the curse could be broken only by one of Adam's children. Jesus was uniquely qualified. A descendent of Adam through Mary, His mother, and yet the Son of God at the same time, He dealt conclusively with death by taking in it into His own body. Thus the death of the Lord of life was the death of death itself. He *has destroyed death and brought life and immortality to light through the gospel,* writes St. Paul (2 Tim. 1:10). Similarly, the letter to the Hebrews elaborates: *Since the children have flesh and blood, he too shared in their humanity so that by his death he might destroy him who holds the power of death–that is, the devil* (2:14).

In the cross, the tyranny of Satan was broken. The old ancient foe met his defeat. The deceiver was deceived, the accuser stood accused, and the destroyer was destroyed. On His cross, Jesus undid all the havoc wreaked by the devil at Eden's tree.

An ancient liturgical preface captures the irony of God's battle strategy, contrasting the source of death with its antidote. The comparison is somewhat cryptic, but vivid:

> That, whence death arose, thence Life also might rise again; and that he who by a tree once overcame might likewise by a tree be overcome.

In the Garden of Eden Satan had overcome Adam by a tree. But on the tree of the cross the New Adam overthrew Satan. An instrument of death became the instrument of life.

As it was at the cross, so it is in the baptismal font. In the cross, the wood that had destroyed mankind in Eden became our victory at Calvary. So also in Baptism: the very water that destroys brings new life. Drowning becomes rebirth.

The Victor's Command

Fresh from the grave, where He defeated sin, death, and hell, the risen Lord gave instructions to His followers. No longer were they *disciples*, or students. From now on they would be known as *apostles*, or sent ones—His personal agents. *"All authority in heaven and on earth has been given to me,* He said. *Therefore go and make disciples of all nations, baptizing them in the name of the Father and of the Son and of the Holy Spirit"* (Matt. 28:18–19). "Baptize" means "wash." Water, in other words, applied by Christ's personal representatives under the authority of God Himself, would be the initiating agent in enrolling new disciples. The water of Baptism would be the agent of life for believers because it was also the agent of death for sin.

Our Watery Grave

The Bible is rich in baptismal imagery that clarifies the meaning and impact of Christian Baptism. One theme is the Red Sea victory.

St. Paul identifies the defeat of Pharaoh at the Red Sea as a prototype of Baptism. *For I do not want you to be ignorant of the fact, brothers, that our forefathers were all under the cloud and that they all passed through the sea. They were all baptized into Moses in the cloud and in the sea* (1 Cor. 10:1–2). The dramatic narrative of the Pharaoh's defeat is found in Exodus 12–15. The drowning of the tyrant's army begins with the Passover, the meal of deliverance from death that Jesus used as the foundation for His Supper. Thus both of these Sacraments find a common origin in deliverance from death in the face of death. More about that later.

For now, please note this irony: the very same water that destroyed Pharaoh and his army was also Israel's salvation. While they walked through the sea unscathed, Pharaoh and his troops were utterly wiped out, and God won the victory:

> The Lord said to Moses: . . . "Lift up your rod, and stretch out your hand over the sea and divide it, that the people of Israel may go on dry ground through the sea. And I will harden the hearts of the Egyptians so that they shall go in after them, and I will get glory over Pharaoh and all his host, his chariots, and his horsemen. And the Egyptians shall know that I am the LORD, when I have gotten glory over Pharaoh, his chariots, and his horsemen." (Ex. 14:15–17)

This was not simply a military victory, St. Paul informs us. The Israelites were all *baptized into Moses* as they passed through the sea (1 Cor. 10:2) It's interesting that he uses exactly the same terminology to describe the Sacrament of Christian Baptism: *baptized into Christ* (Gal. 3:27). It appears that there's a connection between the life-giving Sacrament of Holy Baptism and the "baptism" Israel received at the Red Sea.

Consider these parallels: As Moses led the escape from Pharaoh, so Jesus leads His people out from the tyranny of Satan. The name *Moses* refers to his adoption out of water, according to Ex. 2:10. Jesus' name, on the other hand, is the Aramaic equivalent of "Joshua," the Old Testament successor to Moses. His name means "The Lord Saves." It's as though we have a drama in two acts: *God Delivers His People*. First it's Moses, Israel, and the Red Sea. Then it's Jesus, the church, and Baptism. The Old Testament sets the stage, and the New Testament provides the resolution. The first act foreshadows the second. God delivers His people through water.

The water that saved Israel was deadly to Pharaoh and his troops. So also the baptismal washing ultimately leads to life, but first passes through death. *All of us who were baptized into Christ,* writes St. Paul, *were baptized into his death[.] We were therefore buried with him through baptism into death in order that, just as Christ was raised from the dead through the glory of the Father, we too may live a new life* (Rom. 6:3–4). In the mention of Jesus' resurrection by the "glory of the Father" we hear an echo of the glory achieved by God in the drowning of Pharaoh and his army.

Christ's victory means Satan's defeat. And this victory/defeat is personally applied to every believer in his Baptism. It's no accident that the church to this day precedes Baptism with the renunciation of Satan and all his works and all his ways. We all come into this world as slaves of sin, death, and hell. In the waters of Holy Baptism we are set free from slavery; we share in the victory Christ won by His cross. But that victory comes out of death. And the same Baptism which raises us to life first plunges us into death. This is precisely why there is life in this water; like the water of the Red Sea, it brings life by destroying the enemy. When we pass through the waters of Baptism a death occurs. It is the same death Christ died long ago: *The death he died, he died to sin once for all; but the life he lives, he lives to God* (Rom. 6:10).

In Baptism our sins are buried with Christ, and we die to sin. Thus our Baptism is our grave. A grave like Pharaoh's—a watery grave.

A Consignment Deal

We have seen in the previous chapter how Jesus assumed our sins by His Baptism at the Jordan by John. There He was given over into death just as surely as the day He took up His cross and headed for Calvary. Our Baptism begins with the Baptism of Jesus, where He stepped into His saving work by that washing of repentance for the forgiveness of sins. The Holy Spirit descended on Him like a dove, calling to mind the dove that appeared at the conclusion of the deluge in Noah's day. Then the Father's voice affirmed Him and His saving work: *"You are my Son, whom I love; with you I am well pleased"* (Mark 1:11). The Baptism of Jesus, in other words, was a seal and affirmation of His saving work. That Baptism was His consignment into our death.

And it works the other way around, too. As Jesus was baptized into our death, so we are baptized into His death. Our death meant death for Him, but His death means life for us. Consigned into His death by Baptism, we are partners with Him in His risen life. Thus Baptism is at once our tomb and our mother, as the ancient church fathers continually reminded the faithful. Holy Baptism is both our tomb of death and our womb of life.

Alive in Christ

Our baptismal link with Jesus in His death lies behind St. Paul's repeated use of the phrase "in Christ." Because we have shared with Him in His death by Baptism, we also share with Him in His resurrection. Because we were buried with Him by Baptism into death we now share in Christ's own risen life. We were given over by our Baptism into the death of Jesus and the resurrection of Jesus. And if we have been given over into the death and resurrection of Jesus, we are given over into Jesus Himself. Hence every baptized believer now lives "in Christ."

This is not just a figure of speech, nor is it simply a pet expression of the apostle Paul. The New Testament makes it abundantly clear that the believer's life is not his own; he lives in Christ as Christ lives in him. That is, Jesus actually lives out His own life through every baptized child of God. Since *you who were baptized into Christ have clothed yourselves with Christ* (Gal. 3:27), we can truthfully say: *I have been crucified with Christ and I no longer live, but Christ lives in me. The life I live in the body, I live by faith in the Son of God, who loved me and gave himself for me* (2:20).

And Jesus Himself is the real power at work in our life. *"I am the vine,"* Jesus pointed out, *"you are the branches. If a man remains in me and I in him, he will bear much fruit; apart from me you can do nothing"* (John 15:5). By Baptism we are grafted into Christ, by Baptism we live in Christ. And when we live in Christ, we really live!

Human willpower is notoriously anemic and fickle. Jesus Christ, on the other hand, is firm, steady, and sure. I wonder—do you suppose the reason you and I have such a hard time living the Christian life is that we try to go it alone, apart from our Baptism into Christ? Baptismal renewal happens as we confess our sins and return in repentance to the forgiveness of sins we first received in Baptism, where we were joined to Christ and His risen life. Small wonder that St. Paul would say, *For to me, to live is Christ* (Phil. 1:21). We simply cannot live apart from the life we have in Him by our Baptism into Him.

The ancient church described baptized believers as fish, conceived in water, born to swim in water. And you know what happens to fish out of water.

A New Creation

I mentioned that the New Testament sees the defeat of Pharaoh at the Red Sea as a prototype of Baptism. As water was the agent of destruction, so it was also the agent of salvation. The same water that drowns the sinner brings forth the new man in Christ. And by mentioning "a new man," we're confronted with an even more vivid prototype of Baptism, which is the Creation and the Flood.

"Behold, I will create new heavens and a new earth," God said through His Old Testament prophet, Isaiah (65:17). What God will bring about ultimately on the Last Day He has already begun in Christ. We can see this most clearly in the opening lines of the Gospel of John, where the first words of Genesis are echoed:

> In the beginning was the Word, and the Word was with God, and the Word was God. . . . Through him all things were made; without him nothing was made that has been made. . . . The Word became flesh and made his dwelling among us. We have seen his glory, the glory of the One and Only, who came from the Father, full of grace and truth. (John 1:1, 3, 14)

In Genesis, God made the world by His powerful word: *let there be*. In Jesus Christ, this eternal Word from the Father has taken up residence in human flesh. Jesus Christ is the beginning of God's new creation. Throughout the gospels we see Him at work, undoing the effects of sin: healing the sick, giving sight to the blind, casting out demons. *"If I drive out demons by the Spirit of God,"* He informed his enemies, *"then the kingdom of God has come upon you"* (Matt. 12:28).

61

Jesus Christ is the beginning of the new creation. And by Baptism, He regenerates fallen sinners to be partakers of His new creation. *"I tell you the truth,"* Jesus said to Nicodemus, *"no one can enter the kingdom of God unless he is born of water and the spirit. Flesh gives birth to flesh, but the Spirit gives birth to spirit"* (John 3:5–6).

As the Spirit of God hovered over the chaotic waters of the first creation (Gen. 1:2) and gave life to breathless dust (2:7), so also the Spirit descended at the Jordan where Christ was baptized into our death. According to John, the Baptism of Jesus would be a baptism *with the Holy Spirit* (Mark 1:8). In other words, it was to be a life-giving baptism. And it is. Our Baptism into Christ is truly the water of life. For in this water we have a share in the life of Jesus Christ and His new creation. *He saved us,* St. Paul says, *through the washing of rebirth and renewal by the Holy Spirit, whom he poured out on us generously through Jesus Christ our Savior* (Titus 3:5–6).

The Giver of Life

"The Spirit gives life," said Jesus (John 6:63). As it was in the beginning, so it is now. The same Spirit who brought order out of chaos and turned lifeless clay into living, breathing flesh continues His life-giving work. In Holy Baptism God gives new birth by water and the Spirit. Thus Baptism is the beginning of a radically new life: *If anyone is in Christ, he is a new creation; the old has gone, the new has come* (2 Cor. 5:17).

A New Beginning

By Baptism into Christ we have a whole new life ahead of us. Our old life has disappeared—baptized, dead, and buried into the death of the Crucified One. A new man emerges from that watery grave. Joined with our risen Lord, we rise to live a new life in Him. Each day is a new beginning in Him. The trite phrase of popular folklore finds deeper reality in Holy Baptism: "Today is the first day of the rest of your life." We are a new creation by water and the Spirit.

St. Peter suggests that if we want to understand the new creation God accomplishes in Holy Baptism by water and the Spirit, we ought to look back in history to Noah's day and to the ark he built:

> In it only a few people, eight in all, were saved through water, and this water [points toward] baptism that now saves you also—not the removal of dirt from the body but the pledge of a good conscience toward God. It saves you by the resurrection of Jesus Christ. (1 Peter 3:20–21)

"Noah's flood," we call that deluge. But it really wasn't. It was God's flood. And this flood of water flowed from a flood of grief and pain deep within the very heart of the Creator. His fatherly heart grieved over the wickedness of the creatures He had made.

> The LORD saw how great man's wickedness on the earth had become, and that every inclination of the thoughts of his heart was only evil all the time. The LORD was grieved that he had made man on the earth, and his heart was filled with pain. (Gen. 6:5–6)

And so God started over. As it was in the beginning, so it was again. Once God had called forth light and life out of the chaos of darkness on the face of the great deep. In six days He made the earth and every living thing, resting on the seventh day. And now again the great drama unfolded. Demolition, then construction. The waters held in check at the first creation were unleashed in Noah's day. A great chaotic flood was the agent of God's new creation. New life out of water once more, but first destruction in the Flood. And a destructive flood it was, drowning everything on the face of the whole earth that had the breath of life—with one exception.

A tiny ship floated on the surface of the water. Inside, a male and female of every living species were preserved alive. Within that ark, the Creator lovingly preserved the seeds of life for His new creation. That ark was a colony of life on a sea of death.

Finally the waters receded, and the ark was grounded. For 40 days Noah and his family waited inside with their menagerie. Then he released a dove to see if it was safe to disembark. Finding no place to perch, the dove returned to the ark.

> [Noah] waited seven more days and again sent out the dove from the ark. When the dove returned to him in the evening, there in its beak was a freshly plucked olive leaf! Then Noah knew that the water had receded from the earth. He waited seven more days

and sent the dove out again, but this time it did not return to him.
(Gen. 8:10–12)

On the Eighth Day

It was the same as it was in the beginning, yet different. Originally it took six days to make the earth, the seventh day a sacred day of rest. But this time it took seven days for life to begin again. And on the eighth day Noah and his family—eight in all—disembarked with their little colony of life. A new creation to replenish the earth with living creatures.

The number eight has been associated with Baptism from the earliest days of the church. Ancient sanctuaries were built as octagons, echoing the design of free-standing baptisteries from still earlier times. To this day, many baptismal fonts are constructed with eight sides. Our Christian ancestors knew what they were doing. For eight is the number of the new creation. And by Baptism we are newly created to live in the risen life of Christ.

The third day He rose again from the dead, the church has confessed down through the ages. The resurrection of Jesus Christ from the grave of His death "on the third day" has always been the fundamental reality on which Christians base their faith in the forgiveness of sins, the resurrection of the body, and the life everlasting.

Jesus rose from the dead on the third day of His burial, and that day began a new week. The four evangelists are careful to point out that the women went to embalm his body at dawn after the Sabbath was over, i.e., "on the first day of the week" (Luke 24:1). But the tomb was empty. And so God's new creation in His risen Son began after seven days. Add it up: 7 + 1 = 8. The time of this world was transcended and transformed that day. The first day of the week is thus the eighth day of creation and at the same time the first day of the new creation.

Once again the drama unfolds. The flood of Noah's day and the waters of Baptism are different acts in the same production. As God drowned sin in the Flood, so He drowns our sinful nature by Holy Baptism. But the same water that destroyed all other life lifted the ark safely above. So also the water of Baptism, the agent of death to the Old Adam, is the agent of life for the new man. And we have shelter in this dying world. As Noah and his family were preserved safely in their wooden ship, so the church is our ark of refuge in a raging world, preserved in safety by a cross of wood.

Thus Holy Baptism is our new beginning in the new creation. On the eighth day a dove soared free, eight people stepped out on dry land, and the world began again. It was a foreshadowing of the real thing. For on the eighth day Jesus stepped out of death into life, the first day of the new creation. And the drama continues to unfold, right into our very lives. For in Baptism we are joined to the risen Lord. We too rise from death into life. Baptism is our personal eighth day, the beginning of our new creation as sons and daughters of the risen King.

And the world begins again for us right there—in the baptismal water. And there is life in that water. It is the life of Jesus Christ.

Radical Surgery

God has always been at work bringing life out of death. Abram and his wife, Sarai, became parents long after their child-bearing years were over: *his body was as good as dead,* and *Sarah's womb was also dead,* is St. Paul's droll comment (Rom. 4:19). Yet Abram believed God's promise that He would father a child by his wife.

As an outward mark of that faith of his, God gave Abram circumcision, a surgical sign of God's promise of life out of death. He and his wife were given new names as well. He was no longer Abram, "father"—he was to be called Abraham, "father of many nations." And God said that Sarai was now named Sarah, "princess," *"for I will bless her so that she will be the mother of nations; kings of peoples will come from her"* (Gen. 17:16).

Father Abraham, we call him. But that's not the way it started out. He could not father a child, and Sarah could not conceive one. But God intervened, and this old man and his barren wife became the parents of a son—and through that son, a whole nation: Israel, God's own people. New life was created out of dead flesh.

And in his body—on his very manhood—Abraham bore the intimate mark of God—the sign and seal of His promise of life. Thus circumcision became the sign of a new creation among all the sons of Abraham.

65

> "For the generations to come every male among you who is eight days old must be circumcised. . . . My covenant in your flesh is to be an everlasting covenant." (Gen. 17:12–13)

And so God decreed that baby boys were to be circumcised on the eighth day. Another coincidence? I don't think so.

Noah stepped out of the ark on the eighth day with his family of eight. Jesus stepped out of His grave on the eighth day. And you and I step out of the death of our sinful nature on the day of our Baptism into Christ, which is our personal eighth day—the first day of our new creation in Christ. And our baptismal day is the first day of the rest of our life to all eternity. It is a circumcision to end all circumcisions.

For in Baptism God continues to do radical surgery. It is a circumcision, but not physically. This one is for females as well as males, and it cuts deeply. It removes sin, not merely skin. In Christ all our sin was removed once *and* for all. His death for the sins of the world was the ultimate in circumcisions. Thus Baptism is not just skin deep. It cuts far deeper; for it is our co-burial and co-resurrection with Christ Himself.

> In him you were also circumcised, in the putting off of the sinful nature, not with a circumcision done by the hands of men but with the circumcision done by Christ, having been buried with him in baptism and raised with him through your faith in the power of God, who raised him from the dead. (Col. 2:11–12)

The Sign of the Cross

This is not the place to discuss all the historic ceremonies connected with Christian Baptism. But we could perhaps mention just one: the sign of the cross. In my liturgical tradition, we say to the candidate, "Receive the sign of the holy cross both upon your forehead and upon your heart to mark you as one redeemed by Christ the crucified," twice tracing the shape of the cross upon his body as we speak.

One could argue, of course, that such liturgical traditions are neither commanded nor forbidden in the Scriptures and add nothing to the validity of Baptism. At the same time, however, Christians through the ages have found great comfort and strength in this outward action—for it is strong testimony to the inward reality connected with Baptism. This Sacrament is a sign and seal of the grace of God even more completely than circumcision was a mark of God's promise under the old Abrahamic covenant.

Baptism is our co-death, co-burial, and co-resurrection with Christ. Crucified, dead, and buried, our Old Adam is put to death in Baptism, and a new man emerges to live a new life in connection with Christ. In a real way, it marks the beginning of a marriage made in heaven:

> Christ loved the church and gave himself up for her to make her holy, cleansing her by the washing with water through the word, and to present her to himself as a radiant church, without stain or wrinkle or any other blemish, but holy and blameless. (Eph. 5:25–27)

We have already seen how after Christ's death on the cross blood and water flowed from the wound in His side. That death marks the new creation of His earthly bride, the church. It is the reality prefigured long ago in Eden. There Eve, the mother of all living, was created from the side of her husband, Adam. But this dramatic marriage pales alongside a deeper nuptial union: Christ, the New Adam, creates the church, His holy bride, by the washing of water through the Word. His physical body is the source of life for the church. The blood and water gushing from His side on His cross continues to bring His life to the church in every age. He nourishes and cares for His holy bride, *for we are members of his body, of His flesh and of His bones.* (Eph. 5:30).

No wonder, then, that the sign of the cross has been connected with Baptism from earliest times. The cross of Christ is the source of life for the church—both her origin and her nourishment. In other words, the cross is a mark of ownership as well as protection.

In ancient times, soldiers were given a "seal"—a type of tattoo—when they were enlisted for battle. It was the insignia of their commanding officer on their hand or forehead. Similarly, slaves were given a seal of ownership, which marked their identity.

Scriptural references to a sign or seal include Rev. 9:4, where we are told that the plagues of the final judgment fall on those people *who did not have the seal of God on their foreheads.* A similar idea is found in Ezek. 9:4, where the penitent faithful in Jerusalem are marked on their foreheads, and so escape death. And Cain was given a sign as his protection: *the LORD put a mark on Cain so that no one who found him would kill him* (Gen. 4:15).

But all these signs seem to be visible signs. Why then is the sign of the cross in Holy Baptism simply traced in outline? Because the true gift in Baptism is invisible to the naked eye:

> And you also were included in Christ when you heard the word of truth, the gospel of your salvation. Having believed, you were marked in him with a seal, the promised Holy Spirit, who is a deposit guaranteeing our inheritance until the redemption of those who are God's possession—to the praise of his glory. (Eph. 1:13–14)

A dove was released on the eighth day of creation's new beginning in the days of Noah. The Holy Spirit descended like a dove at the Baptism of Jesus. And in our Baptism we receive the Spirit Himself, who is the seal of divine ownership and protection for us. This seal, though invisible to the eye, is nevertheless indelible. The Spirit's seal is the sign of the cross of Christ.

From the day of our Baptism we are marked indelibly with the life-giving power of the Holy Spirit. We live now as members of the body of Christ, His holy bride, the church. We are marked with the signet seal of His love: *Place me like a seal over your heart, like a seal over your arm; for love is as strong as death* (Song of Songs 8:6).

So Christians through the centuries have cherished the sign of the cross as an ongoing reminder of baptismal identity. Upon rising from sleep, upon going to bed, when eating, and when beginning prayer, many Christians trace the sign of the cross on themselves as they repeat the Word once spoken at their baptismal washing: *in the name of the Father and of the Son and of the Holy Spirit* (Matt. 28:19).

And there is comfort in that sign. For the sign of the cross of Christ is the sign of His love. And that sign is a protecting shield. For where the Lover is, there is protection for the beloved.

> Spread your protection over them, that those who love your name may rejoice in you. For surely, O LORD, you bless the righteous; you surround them with your favor as with a shield. (Ps. 5:11–12)

Eyes to See

Just water, you say? Yes, Holy Baptism is a washing in water. That part you can see with your eyes. But there is a hidden reality as well. This water is the back side of God for us. For wrapped within this water is the Word of God Himself.

Stepping into the Jordan and that bath of repentance for the forgiveness of sins, Jesus Christ consecrated all baptismal water as a *washing of rebirth and renewal by the Holy Spirit* (Titus 3:5). The Jordan runs through every baptismal font. In our Baptism we are given a share in Him who is our life. It is both a sharing in His burial and in His resurrection, in His death and in His life. *The death he died, he died to sin once for all; but the life he lives, he lives to God* (Rom. 6:10).

Consider, then, these things: the water of creation, which was the power of God's creative Word and His life-giving Spirit; the water of the Red Sea, the destruction of Pharaoh and the salvation of Israel; the flood of Noah's day, the destruction of sin and the new creation; the resurrection of Jesus from the dead, the death of sin and the eighth day of God's new creation. Consider circumcision: the mark on Abraham's own body of God's new life. Consider the sign of the cross: the invisible seal of consignment into the death and resurrection of Christ and the indelible mark of His love.

Now look again. You need the eyes of faith to see the hidden reality in Baptism. It is a link with both Jordan and Calvary, river and cross, water and blood. Holy Baptism offers here and now all our Lord accomplished for us then and there. And by faith we receive all He offers.

Baptism is our personal water of life in this dying world, for Baptism is our link with Christ. And there is life in Jesus Christ.

5

Holy Absolution: Word of Life

Confess your sins to each other. (James 5:16)

It was a blue-chip company, and the owner built it from scratch. He had invested his blood and sweat in this enterprise, yet now he announced he was moving on. The managers stared incredulously at each other across the table. No one could imagine operations without him. How would the company carry on?

"If you forgive anyone his sins," said Jesus, "they are forgiven."

Let's Get Real

If you've been reading along faithfully from the beginning of this book, you may be starting to get a bit uneasy. Together we've traced some of the key components in Christian teaching in a way I hope has been fresh and interesting. But you might be getting a little impatient with me by now.

I can almost hear the concerns: "Why does he seem to be going over the same themes again and again?" "What's this constant reference to death and life?" "Why the big emphasis on Baptism?" "Where's the application in all this?"

We are a practical sort of people. We all want to know how an idea affects our lives, what use we can make of it.

That's great, to a point.

But when you and I are confronted by the ancient mysteries of the Christian faith, our good old-fashioned American pragmatism runs up against a brick wall. We ask, "What use can I make of this idea?" But that question doesn't apply. For Christianity is not an idea. It is the one Reality by which all other reality is measured. Christianity is not a way of life; it is life itself. *And this is the testi-*

mony: God has given us eternal life, and this life is in his Son (1 John 5:11).

That's what this book is all about. The Life that is in Jesus Christ. We'd like to know what we can do with this Life, but that's not the issue. The Life that is in Jesus Christ will have its way with us— either to our eternal glory or our eternal shame. This book spotlights the Life Jesus Christ offers here and now in His Word and Sacrament for the glories to come.

And believe me, there's nothing more practical in all the world. We ask whether the holy mysteries of the faith are fiction. But there's nothing more real in all the world. It's just that these are hidden realities.

And that's the focus of this chapter. The hidden life. The connection between reality as we see it and reality as it actually is in Jesus Christ. The realities of our sin, suffering, and pain and the realities of His forgiveness, comfort, and healing. Holy Absolution is the link between Baptism and everyday living.

For many Christians this chapter will seem like a foreign language. Please bear with me. It may be foreign to some of us, but I'm convinced it's our native tongue.

Under the Cross

Life and death. These are the two realities in which we live as baptized children of God. We bear the sign and the seal of the crucified Lord; we are marked with His cross. Buried with Jesus by our Baptism into His death, we are also risen with Him into His new life. This reality of life in the face of death is the essence of Christianity. But in this world it remains a hidden reality. For now we live by faith.

One thing is clear. Since Christianity is a matter of both life and death, those who hope for a life of ease as a child of God deceive themselves. The Lord of life has entered this world of death, and that means there's a life-and-death struggle going on in this dying world of ours. Jesus Christ makes it clear that everyone baptized into Him will live the life of a combat soldier. The entire Christian life in this world is lived on a battlefield. Christ has won the victory, to be sure. But that victory remains hidden to human eyes for now. *For you died, and your life is now hidden with Christ in God. When Christ, who is your life, appears, then you also will appear with him in glory* (Col. 3:3–4).

One day, when God rings down the curtain on the entire drama, these hidden realities will be evident to all. But not now. For now, we live by faith. And since we live by faith, our life in this world bears the sign of the cross.

The cross of Christ cuts two ways, since it is a matter of both life and death. First, it means the life of Jesus Christ in exchange for death. Therefore His cross is our joy and hope. But the cross that brings us the life of Christ also means the death of our sinful nature. And death is never a pleasant experience. Through hardship and affliction, our Lord leads us to take a hard look at our sin, which means He leads us to sorrow and repentance.

This is where you and I usually bail out. It's okay as long as things are going along fine in our lives, but when the going gets tough we often say, "Thanks, Jesus, but no thanks. This is where I get off." Yet our Lord makes it clear that tough sledding is to be expected in the Christian's life: *"If anyone would come after me, he must deny himself and take up his cross and follow me"* (Matt. 16:24).

How easily we forget! The cross of Christ is God's life-giving instrument. There was no way to life for Him except through death. Christ's way is by definition the way of the cross. But it is not our natural way. Left to ourselves, you and I continually choose the path of glory; we'd much rather have strength, power, and prestige than weakness, suffering, and affliction. Yet only one route leads to life. Our way promises life, yet finally delivers only death. Christ's way leads right through death into life. The way of the cross is the only road to life in this dying world.

Targeting the Enemy

We keep missing that road because we keep fighting the wrong battles. The problem is always somebody else, we like to think. If our boss would just get off our back, we'd be a lot happier. If our spouse would lighten up, our life would be worth living. If our circumstances would change, we'd be less angry and bitter.

We even use the same line of thinking in our relationship with God. We're convinced we could straighten ourselves out if only we didn't have to contend with the temptation around us. If we could just clean up the moral cesspool we live in, we're sure we could live God-pleasing lives.

But nothing could be farther from the truth. The Bible makes it clear that our predicament is not the situation we live in, but what lives in us. Our circumstances aren't the problem; our sinful heart is the culprit. Jesus makes it clear that if we want to identify our real enemy, we'll have to look in a mirror: *"For out of the heart come evil thoughts, murder, adultery, sexual immorality, theft, false testimony, slander"* (Matt. 15:19).

The Old Adam

Collectively, these things make up an ugly package. But since we usually see only one or two of the tamer evils cropping up in our life at any given time, we're not very alarmed. Pride, jealousy, greed, and hatred are only natural, we like to think. We call this "human nature." But God calls it sin.

And it's as old as the Garden of Eden. There Adam and Eve caved in to the devil's ploy and joined his rebellion against their Creator. "The Fall" is what we call that first sin of our first parents. It's an apt description, for in that one sin all mankind had a great fall. And just like Humpty Dumpty, we've never been able to put ourselves back together again.

In Adam all die, is the way St. Paul puts it (1 Cor. 15:22). That is, every child of Adam and Eve inherits a fatal flaw. Since the fall into sin, all children born to human parents come into this world with sin engraved deeply in their hearts. And there are no exceptions to this ugly reality: *Like the rest, we were by nature objects of wrath* (Eph. 2:3). Thus our problem before God is not merely the sins we do, but the sinners that we are; sin penetrates our very heart.

The New Man

Yet in His baptismal washing, Jesus Christ gives a new identity. *Therefore, if anyone is in Christ, he is a new creation; the old has gone, the new has come* (2 Cor. 5:17). It should be stressed that this new life is not simply a new way of life, as if Christianity were a cosmetic adjustment of our lifestyle, to bring it into line with God's expectations.

Sin, after all, cannot be reformed or remodeled. The only way to terminate sin is to kill it. And that's precisely what God has done in His Son, Jesus Christ. He is the great Terminator. He bore our sin in His own body, and it killed Him. But in dying He destroyed death, and brought life and immortality to light. In rising from His grave He has shattered the power of the grave. In His resurrection from death He has broken the stranglehold of sin on mankind. In Jesus Christ one of Adam's sons escaped the fate of Adam's children. *For we know that since Christ was raised from the dead, he cannot die again; death no longer has mastery over him* (Rom. 6:9).

And the good news is that by Baptism into Christ, every believer participates in His death and resurrection. *Or don't you know that all of us who were baptized into Christ Jesus were baptized into his death? We were therefore buried with him through baptism into death in order that, just as Christ was raised from the dead through the glory of the Father, we too may live a new life* (Rom. 6:3–4).

Holy Baptism is thus both a doorway and a hinge. It is the doorway to a whole new life. And it is also the hinge upon which that way of life depends. Both the new life and the new way of life are one reality: the life Jesus Christ lives out through His people.

Sworn Enemies

In some church circles the Baptism of adults is viewed as something they do to affirm their faith in Jesus. In other churches the Baptism of infants is regarded as a quaint family custom. Both views are inadequate. In fact, they're dead wrong. Baptism is never a human activity; it is God's work, done *in the name of the Father and of the Son and of the Holy Spirit* (Matt. 28:19).

And there is nothing customary or quaint about Baptism. Baptism means the death of the Old Adam and the resurrection of the new man. There's nothing more radical than death and resurrection.

We do no one any favors when we baptize him into the strong name of the Triune God. For every baptized child of God bears the sign and seal of the cross, the mark of a soldier serving under the Crucified One. And the enemy means business. The devil is the sworn enemy of God and all the works of God. His unswerving goal is to devastate God's people and destroy God's kingdom.

The Struggle

So which is it, we wonder. Am I a child of God or a child of Satan? Am I a servant of righteousness or a slave of sin? Am I saint or sinner?

The scriptural answer is a frustrating yes. In this world every Christian is both saint and sinner, servant and slave, child and rebel. We'd like to think that a Christian should be able to rid his life of sin. Whole books are written as "do it yourself" manuals for victory over sin.

Yet the Bible makes it clear that there's only one victory over sin: the victory Jesus Christ has already won on His cross. One day, in heaven's glory, we will be completely free of sin. Here we live only and entirely by faith in Jesus Christ, who frees us from sin in the Word of His Gospel.

In the Apostles' Creed, the church confesses three glorious realities: the forgiveness of sins, the resurrection of the body, and the life everlasting. The first reality makes the other two possible. The forgiveness of sins is the church's daily bread and butter. We have no life with God apart from the forgiveness of sins. And we have hope for Judgment Day and eternity only because we live constantly in the reality of the forgiveness of our sins.

For our lives are a battleground. Daily a battle wages between our Old Adam and the new man, between our sinful nature and the new nature we have by Baptism into Christ. The new man is controlled by Christ and seeks to serve God alone. The Old Adam is driven by selfish pride, intent on feeding our own sinful desires.

And so our predicament is just as Pogo put it: "We have met the enemy, and he is us." But this dilemma is no joke.

> I know that nothing good lives in me, that is, in my sinful nature. For I have the desire to do what is good, but I cannot carry it out. For what I do is not the good I want to do; no, the evil I do not want to do—this I keep on doing. Now if I do what I do

75

not want to do, it is no longer I who do it, but it is sin living in me that does it. (Rom. 7:18–20)

The Final Solution

There's only one way to deal with sin. Not by reform, but by death and resurrection. Not by remodeling, but by demolition and reconstruction. As the Old Adam dies, the new man emerges and arises. The forgiveness of sins is essentially a repeat performance of the mighty drama God unfolded once for all in the death and resurrection of His Son and then personally and individually for every believer in Baptism.

Remember, resurrection is always a new creation. And God accomplishes His new creation as He did the first creation: by His almighty Word. Then He spoke into the formless void to bring forth light and life by the power of His Word. Now He still works as He did at the beginning: *For God, who said, "Let light shine out of darkness," made his light shine in our hearts to give us the light of the knowledge of the glory of God in the face of Christ* (2 Cor. 4:6). Thus the same creative Word of God is the common power behind our new creation in Holy Baptism and behind our ongoing renewal in the forgiveness of our sins.

But here, too, we have a problem. For we all know that as new creations of God it is our duty to lead holy lives and serve Him with works of love. *For we are God's workmanship, created in Christ Jesus to do good works, which God prepared in advance for us to do* (Eph. 2:10). The question is, why are we so inept in our good works and anemic in our struggle against sin?

Remember the early church's illustration: Christians are fish, born in water to swim in water. Perhaps our problem is our do-it-yourself approach to Christian living, attempting to overcome sin on the basis of our own willpower. After all, you know what happens to fish out of water.

Remembering Baptism

I used to think that the key to leading a sanctified (holy) life was my own willpower. I needed to get a good grip on myself and simply try harder, I thought. "Remember your Baptism," I was told. "Remember who you are as a baptized child of God and then simply lead a holy life accordingly." It sounded good, but it didn't work. Try as I might, firm resolutions and good intentions just didn't do the trick. To tell me to try harder was like telling a sick person to act well. Thankfully, God provided stronger medicine.

My advisors were right. Holy Baptism is the hinge upon which the holy life depends—not simply as an event from the past, but as a present reality. *For as many of you as were baptized into Christ have put on Christ,* writes St. Paul (Gal. 3:27 RSV). Here the apostle makes it clear that the past action of Baptism has ongoing implications.

Baptism, you remember, means consignment into the death and resurrection of Jesus Christ. Jesus Christ takes the sinner, sins and all, with Him into His death and buries him in His grave. Thus St. Paul can call Holy Baptism *a likeness of His death* (Rom. 6:5 KJV). In Baptism a death occurs. It is the death of our Old Adam. And out of this watery grave a new man emerges. *I have been crucified with Christ and I no longer live, but Christ lives in me* (Gal. 2:20). This new man newly created is constantly being renewed *in the image of its Creator* (Col. 3:10).

The Naked Truth

All of this sounds abstract. True, these things are hidden truths, but they are real, just the same. I've discovered there's nothing more practical and vividly real than the new life Christ bestows on everyone baptized into His name. And this is the key to the sanctified life; not simply "remembering" Baptism by thinking about a fact from our past, but living out of the hidden realities first worked in our lives by this *washing of rebirth and renewal by the Holy Spirit* (Titus 3:5).

A radical change has taken place in Baptism, which the New Testament variously calls a death and burial (Rom. 6:3), a crucifixion (Gal. 2:20), and a stripping and reclothing (Gal. 3:27). It should be stressed that this is God's action, not the believer's. And that makes it all the more radical.

77

In Eden, the first thing Adam and Eve did after their rebellion was to hide their nakedness behind fig leaves (Gen. 3:7). And immediately after promising deliverance to His fallen children, *the Lord God made garments of skin for Adam and his wife and clothed them* (3:21). This leather clothing could cover their bodies, but it could not cover their sin. In Holy Baptism God delivers what He first promised in the Garden. We are stripped bare of our Old Adam and clothed in Jesus Christ Himself.

Interestingly enough, early Christian Baptisms routinely included the stripping off of old clothing, Baptism in the nude, and postbaptismal vesting in a new white garment. Rooms set aside for such private baptismal bathing were frequently decorated with mosaics depicting the original paradise of Eden. Thus a church daily under fire impressed upon its faithful the hidden realities behind the sacred mystery of baptism:

- Baptism is stripping off the Old Adam.
- Baptism is the death and burial of sin.
- Baptism is a return to Eden and innocence before God.
- Baptism is the resurrection of the new man.
- Baptism is putting on the perfection of Jesus Christ.

A Radical Proposal

I'm not suggesting that Baptisms be conducted the same way today; it's always dangerous to run a church by archeology. We are not interested in reviving ancient traditions for their own sake. But these practices flowed from the same apostolic Gospel we have today. And if we have eyes to see it, we will find today the same living, vibrant reality in Holy Baptism our early brothers and sisters in the faith found in their era.

As these hidden realities began to dawn on me, I came to see the New Testament—indeed all of Holy Scripture—not as a "do it yourself" manual for Christian living, but rather the divinely inspired proclamation of what God has done *and continues to do* in His Son, Jesus Christ. I began to see that no matter where you open up the New Testament, you get very wet. That is, the entire Christian gospel is saturated with baptismal teaching. The moral implications of the Christian gospel are already implied in Baptism. And the new life we live as Christians is nothing more than applied Baptism.

The contrast with current popular Christian teaching is striking. The so-called principles for Christian living so prevalent in Christian bestsellers and so prominent among Christian media teachers are at best a dim parody of the Christian life presented in the Scriptures.

The truth is, all of the New Testament's imperatives are based on its indicatives. In other words, everything God demands of His children He first gives His children. Everything God wants us to do He has already done in His Son, and He continues to work in us in and through Jesus Christ. He is not a departed hero gone off to heaven to watch how well we're doing here on earth without Him. He is present here and now with His church in those sacred mysteries we call the Word and the Sacraments. There's a link between the life Christians lead and their living Lord. And that link is Baptism.

People keep looking for the key to a dynamic Christian life, some magic formula to bring zest to dull, half-hearted commitment. Unfortunately, most of the formulas suggested tend to be do-it-yourself projects. A do-it-yourself approach to the Christian life is doomed from the start. Reform a sinner and you get a reformed sinner. Discipline a sinner and you get a disciplined sinner. Educate a sinner and you get an educated sinner. In every case you still have the same sinner you started out with.

No, the Old Adam will not be tamed or reformed or disciplined or educated. He can only be killed. And this is just what God does; in Holy Baptism we are put to death and buried. But since it is the death and burial of Jesus, it makes all the difference in the world. IIis death and burial brings with it resurrection and new life. By Holy Baptism the Triune God crucifies our Old Adam, buries our sin, raises us as a new creation, and clothes us in Jesus Christ— thus giving us a whole new life to live. This is the authentic formula for Christian living!

A Case History

Let me cite one New Testament case history. In Ephesians we

see baptismal teaching applied to a perennial problem—sexual immorality. Then, as now, Christians living in a pagan culture were continually lured to give in to bodily impulses and indulge their selfish sexual appetites. What was the solution? Resolve more firmly to resist? Learn the principles of Christian sexuality and comply accordingly? No, the key for these people was to return to Baptism and to apply what had already happened there when their Old Adam was stripped off and they were clothed in Jesus Christ:

> Now this I affirm and testify in the Lord, that you must no longer live as the Gentiles do, in the futility of their minds; they are darkened in their understanding, alienated from the life of God because of the ignorance that is in them, due to the hardness of heart; they have become callous and have given themselves up to licentiousness, greedy to practice every kind of uncleanness.
>
> You did not so learn Christ!—assuming that you have heard about Him and were taught in Him, as the truth is in Jesus. Put off your old nature which belongs to your former manner of life and is corrupt through deceitful lusts, and be renewed in the spirit of your minds, and put on the new nature, created after the likeness of God in true righteousness and holiness. (Eph. 4:17–24 RSV)

Notice the clear baptismal overtones. The moral imperatives here are based on the indicatives of Baptism. God asks Christians to do what He has already given them. And it's graphic language. "Put off . . . put on" recalls what happened in Baptism when believers were stripped naked of the Old Adam and clothed instead with Jesus Christ.

Here is power for Christian holiness that is more than skin deep. It is the power of Jesus Christ Himself.

Mind Games?

So what is this baptismal living all about, you ask. Isn't this just another variation on the power of positive thinking? Isn't it simply a matter of attitude, "remembering your Baptism" as the basis for self-improvement? Isn't all this talk about Baptism finally just talk, more mind games?

But God doesn't play mind games. He doesn't just give us a new attitude; He gives us a whole new life. He drowns the Old Adam in us by Baptism and creates us new in Jesus Christ. Not just once, but over and over again in the Word of His Gospel. Continually He cleanses us from all sin; He pronounces us "not guilty" by the forgiveness of our sins. When He forgives our sins, He deals death to the Old Adam and raises us to newness of life in Christ.

Freedom From Slavery

"Unfortunately, the Old Adam swims well," Luther once remarked. And every honest Christian agrees. For just when we think we've conquered one sin, another rears its ugly head. And most devastating of all, over and over again we find ourselves falling right back into the very sins we detest the most. It's the same situation St. Paul found himself in:

> So I find this law at work: When I want to do good, evil is right there with me. For in my inner being I delight in God's law; but I see another law at work in the members of my body, waging war against the law of my mind and making me a prisoner of the law of sin at work within my members. What a wretched man I am! Who will rescue me from this body of death? Thanks be to God—through Jesus Christ our Lord! (Rom. 7:21–25)

Thank God, there is still rescue from the guilt and bondage of sin. And it is still a rescue through Jesus Christ, our Lord. He performs this rescue through His called servants in the spoken word of forgiveness, or Holy Absolution.

Out of the Dark Ages?

There's something about the word *absolution* that sounds positively medieval. It conjures up pictures of dark confessional booths and trite penitential formulas. In our enlightened age of education and psychotherapy, confession and absolution seem irrelevant.

"Why would I want to confess my sins to somebody else?" we protest. "I've already confessed them to God! Besides, what I really need is to do something myself about overcoming sin."

81

But that's just the point, isn't it? You and I can't do anything to overcome our own sin. Christ overcomes sin. He won the victory once at Calvary, and He applied that victory to us once in our Baptism. But He extends that victory to us over and over again in the word of His gospel.

The Words of Christ

Liberal Christianity has such a watered down view of the New Testament that it can say very little, if anything, about Jesus of Nazareth with any certainty. In its view, many quotations attributed to Jesus in the Bible actually were made up by various early Christians with a variety of theological axes to grind.

By contrast, fundamentalist Christians have a very high view of the Bible, but an extremely low view of its place in the Christian life. That is, the Bible in their view tends to be seen essentially as a "how to" manual for Christians to receive divine instructions on godly living. It's as though the commanding officer has gone away and left his army with only a set of instructions.

Perhaps it's time to recover a church life and a personal spiritual life built on the real presence of Christ, not His real absence. He has not gone away and left His soldiers to fend for themselves. He's still present with His church in those sacred mysteries which are His word and sacrament.

Words of Power

All reality finally hinges on the Word of God. *"Let there be,"* the Creator spoke, *"and it was so."* And Jesus is the Word of the Father made flesh (John 1:1–17). *"The words I have spoken to you are spirit and they are life,"* He told His contemporaries (John 6:63). In other words, Jesus reminds us that His words have the power to create anything they describe, including the forgiveness of sins.

And He has entrusted those words of His to His church. In His high priestly prayer the night before His execution, Jesus prayed for the disciples He would leave behind as He went to the Father. Yet looking down the corridors of history, He did not pray for these men alone, but also *"for those who will believe in me through their message"* (John 17:20).

Power of Attorney

Jesus was concerned about the welfare of His church on earth. How was she to carry on without His visible presence? In His prayer to the Father that night in Gethsemane, we see the answer:

> "For I gave them the words you gave me and they accepted them. . . . I have given them your word and the world has hated them, for they are not of the world any more than I am of the world. My prayer is not that you take them out of the world but that you protect them from the evil one. They are not of the world, even as I am not of it. Sanctify them by the truth; your word is truth." (John 17:8, 14–17)

Three nights later, on Easter evening, He impressed on His disciples the duty and privilege He was delegating to them even more vividly. Fresh from His grave, the risen Lord stood among His disciples and greeted them: *"Peace to you! As the Father has sent me, I also send you." And when he had said this, he breathed on them and said, "Receive the Holy Spirit. If you forgive the sins of any, they are forgiven; if you retain the sins of any, they are retained"* (John 20:21–23 NKJV).

Notice here the strong connection between the words of Jesus and the life-giving breath of the Spirit of God. Once the Creator had breathed the breath of life into lifeless clay, and Adam became a living soul. Now the New Adam, newly sprung from death, the first man of the new creation, breathes the same life-giving Spirit on His chosen disciples. Apprentices no longer, they are now His commissioned representatives, apostles, "sent ones"—sent by the Son who was sent by the Father to ransom and to rescue His fallen world. That ransom is complete, but the rescue continues in every age—in the powerful Word delivered by those whom the Son has sent.

Christ calls every Christian to be His witness, but He doesn't call every Christian to be His minister, or agent. Through His witnesses Christ bears testimony to all mankind regarding His life for our dying world. But He works uniquely in the church through His ministers for the forgiveness of sins. The church calls pastors from her own midst, but it is Christ Himself who stands behind the office of the ministry. They are earthly agents for our heavenly Lord. He gives His called servants power of attorney, as it were. When they forgive, He forgives. When they withhold forgiveness, He withholds forgiveness. Their word is to be regarded as His word. And His word is the Word from the Father. *"He who receives you receives me, and he who receives me receives the one who sent me"* (Matt. 10:40).

God's Mouth

It was not a novel idea, of course. God did the same thing countless times before. He chose certain spokesmen and then gave them His own word to speak. Take Jeremiah, for instance. When God selected him to be His prophet, Jeremiah was somewhat reluctant because of his youthful inexperience. This was not an obstacle, God showed him:

> Then the LORD reached out his hand and touched my mouth and said to me, "Now, I have put my words in your mouth. See, today I appoint you over nations and kingdoms to uproot and tear down, to destroy and overthrow, to build and to plant." (Jer. 1:9–10)

Notice the vivid emphasis on the oral aspect of Jeremiah's work. The very words of God were placed right into the mouth of Jeremiah. It was a mouth transplant, of sorts. God had given Jeremiah the commission to speak His Word. From then on, whenever he opened his mouth to speak in the name of God, out came the words of God.

Other examples from Scripture could be mentioned. But the point is clear. God has so arranged it in His church that when appointed servants of Christ speak His word of forgiveness, it is to be regarded as Christ's very own Word.

But I still haven't answered the question; why would a Christian want to go to another human being with his sin in the first place?

84

Counseling or Consolation?

One thing's for sure. We don't confess something just to get it "off our chest." There's something in the old adage confession is good for the soul, but there's more to confession and absolution than merely talking out our problems. Thank God for good friends with whom we can unburden our hearts. And thank God for counselors who can give us godly advice.

But confession of sins is not the same as unloading a burden on a friend. And absolution is not the same as good advice. For when we come face to face with sin, we don't need advice. We need forgiveness.

In dealing with the fallout of sin in our lives, we could use all the good advice we can get. Christian counselors can be helpful in redirecting our lives to healthy patterns of behavior. But before we can reform our lives, we need rescue. We need the peace and consolation only Christ can give. And in the private setting of confession and absolution that's exactly what He gives us, uniquely and personally.

There is no one so lonely as someone alone with his sin. But in Holy Absolution Christ abolishes that loneliness. For Christ is present in that brother who hears my confession. And He is with me in my pain. He speaks through the mouth of my brother to erase my guilt in the word of His forgiveness. And in that word there is healing and peace. It is the healing and peace of Christ.

Telling the Truth

It's a simple matter of truth. Left to ourselves, we make excuses for sin. We tell ourselves we had no choice; others were to blame. Sometimes we create a whole fictitious world of our own, rewriting the script of reality. And in that script we're always the starring character. In our view of reality, we're always the hero. The villain is always the other guy.

In that neat little world we've created, it's easy to apply the Gospel to ourselves. For after all, we haven't sinned that badly. There were extenuating circumstances. The devil made me do it. Or my boss. Or my friend. It's always someone else's fault.

And so we take comfort in the Gospel. "Jesus died to free us from sin," we say confidently. And He has. The trouble is, we haven't properly identified the sin, and so the sinner goes on living. But the sinner must die.

That's the trouble when we self-medicate with the Gospel. We can see others' sins, but we can't see our own. The Gospel then becomes an excuse for sin. But when we face our sin openly with our brother and tell the truth before God, the Gospel spells the death of sin and the rebirth of the new man in Christ.

Sound familiar? It ought to. That's what happened first of all in Holy Baptism. There the Old Adam died and the new man was raised. And that's what happens over and over again in Holy Absolution. The Old Adam dies and the new man rises to live a new life. And that new life is the life of Jesus Christ.

The Ugly Truth

There is nothing pleasant about this kind of honesty. There is nothing more painful than to be brutally frank about sin. But then, there is never anything pleasant about death. And telling the truth before God spells the death of our Old Adam, who is always complaining that he's too young to die. So we go on with our little masquerade, pretending our sin is not so bad and that we can handle it on our own.

Thus the ugliness of sin goes on living behind our proud masks of respectability. But we pay a great price for this charade. For it gets lonely living behind a mask. It gets tiring trying to keep our Old Adam at bay. Fending off sin as best we can and trying to lead a godly life by our own willpower is exhausting. We get weary from the sheer struggle of this kind of life. And we should. For we are living a lie, and when you live a lie the deception finally wears you out.

Saying the Truth

The apostle John provides the answer to our exhausting masquerade: *If we claim to be without sin, we deceive ourselves and the truth is not in us. If we confess our sins, he is faithful and just and will forgive us our sins and purify us from all unrighteousness* (1 John 1:8–9).

"Confess" means to "say the same thing." Sometimes in church we confess the faith, usually using the words of an ancient creed. In this case we are "saying the same thing" as our brothers and sisters in Christ, confessing with our lips what we believe in our hearts—confessing the historic faith of the church of all ages.

But when we confess our sins, we "say the same thing" as God. We take an honest look at our sin and in His presence call it exactly what He calls it: death. Christians in my liturgical tradition sometimes say it this way: "I, a poor, miserable sinner, confess to you all my sins and iniquities with which I have ever offended you and justly deserved your punishment now and forever." But no matter which words you use, confession always amounts to the same thing: the truth. The naked, ugly truth. *I know that nothing good lives in me, that is, in my sinful nature* (Rom. 7:18).

Taking Off Our Masks

It's fairly easy to say the words *I am a sinner.* It is quite another thing to confess our sin; that is, to lay it out openly before God in all of its ugliness. That's why we tend to hide our sin. Like Adam and Eve, we hide from God in shame. *"I was afraid,"* Adam said, *"because I was naked; and so I hid myself."* But God is not ashamed of the nakedness of our sin. Remember, Jesus Christ joyfully embraced our shame on the cross so that He could remove it forever. And so there is no shame in sin confessed, no matter how ugly it may be. The only real shame is in trying to live with all that ugliness inside.

But when Christians take off their masks to expose their sin to God in the presence of another, there is healing. For the healing of guilt is a matter of honesty before God. And our confessor, that person who hears our confession, is there to keep us honest. He will be with us as we take off our masks to face our sin in all its horror. But He will also give us the honest truth about sins forgiven in the name of Jesus: they are gone!

That's why, while any Christian can speak the forgiveness of sins, ordinarily we go to our pastors for confession. We're not looking for the sympathetic ear of a friend, after all. And we're not looking for the perceptive insight of a counselor. We're looking for the truth. And so we come before God's servant for God's truth. His ear is God's ear, to hear our sin. But also his mouth is God's mouth, to speak God's forgiveness.

Faithful Christian pastors treat sins confessed to them with utmost confidentiality. There is a sacred seal in confession which deserves to be honored with the strictest secrecy. Why should sins confessed be dredged up from memory ever again? After all, confession is a grave for sins; it is holy ground. Here the heartsick sinner lays bare the ugliness of sin—and by the authority of the risen Lord the pastor addresses that explicit sin with the explicit word of the Gospel.

The pastor's word of forgiveness is the very Word of Christ. This Holy Absolution is therefore baptismal renewal. Sins are buried with Christ. The sinner is cleansed and renewed. The Old Adam dies anew and the new man rises to live again. And the life he lives is not his own. It is the life of Jesus Christ.

The Silent Lie

Blessed is he whose transgressions are forgiven, whose sins are covered, sang David. *Blessed is the man whose sin the* LORD *does not count against him and in whose spirit is no deceit* (Ps. 32:1–2). He knew what he was talking about. For David, the greatest king of ancient Israel, was also one of the greatest sinners of all time.

You can read all about David's sin in 2 Samuel 11. The plot includes pride, lust, adultery, greed, ambition, hatred, and murder. You know that story line; it sounds like a soap opera. But this is not fiction. It really happened. And it happens with a lot of people today just the way it happened with David.

David's sin ultimately had its way with him. And before it was over, it led him to bed with another man's wife, to conspiracy, and an arranged murder. It was an ugly scene. But the ugliest thing of all was what it did to David. David tried to go on living as if nothing had happened.

So David played out his charade. Was he not God's anointed, after all? Was he not the king of God's special people, Israel? Was he not God's great king? And so David carried on his masquerade, pretending he had never sinned. But it didn't work. For he was living a lie. When you live a lie, you live in death. And death takes its toll on you. David can tell you firsthand; listen to his prayer: *When I kept silent, my bones wasted away through my groaning all day long. For day and night your hand was heavy upon me; my strength was sapped as in the heat of summer* (Ps. 32:3–4).

David was the king of Israel and had a court full of admirers, but inside he was all alone, for he was alone with his sin. And so David was a lonely man, if ever there was one.

The Spoken Truth

But not for long. In His mercy, God sent His prophet Nathan to end David's cheap masquerade. No more games. It was time for truth. You can read about the confrontation in 2 Samuel 12. It was a painful confrontation, but then death is never pleasant. And David's sin had to die if he was to really live again.

And that's exactly what happened. David stopped playing games. He took an honest look at his life, and he confessed. He said the same thing as God said about his sin, though that truth was ugly and painful. *Then David said to Nathan, "I have sinned against the LORD." Nathan replied, "The LORD has taken away your sin. You are not going to die"* (2 Sam. 12:13).

Remember who was talking. Nathan was God's prophet, chosen to speak His very Word. Nathan's ear was God's ear to hear David's confession, and Nathan's mouth was God's mouth to speak His absolution.

And that absolution was valid. It was God's truth. After David saw his sin and spit out the ugly truth of that sin, it was time for him to shut his mouth and open up his ears. Now through the mouth of his servant Nathan, God placed His word of forgiveness right into David's eardrums. Then this broken man found healing. It was God's own healing, provided personally for David on the lips of a man.

And so in our brokenness and pain you and I need not be alone. In the sacred seclusion of private confession, we may speak the ugly truth of our sin to God. And in Holy Absolution you and I hear forgiveness from the lips of our pastor. There is power in his words; for they are the very words of Christ. And then we are alone with our sin no longer.

Life Together

God often works like that. Just as He speaks His forgiveness to us through a pastor, He provides His help and consolation in fellowship with others. As we live out our lives under the cross of Jesus Christ, we are not alone. He gives us brothers and sisters in Christ in whose company our burdens are divided and our joys multiplied.

Bear one another's burdens, St. Paul urged, *and so fulfill the law of Christ* (Gal. 6:2 RSV). This "law" is the love of the Lord Jesus Christ, and so it is no law at all. For such love cannot be legislated, it can only be given as a gift. And that's just what happens within the fellowship of the Christian church. Every Christian becomes an arm of the love of Christ, weeping with those who weep and rejoicing with those who rejoice. Now in our tears and in our joy we are no longer alone. For our brother or sister is with us. And in that brother or sister, Christ Himself is present.

What a high privilege it is to extend the love and consolation of Christ! *Each man will be like a shelter from the wind and a refuge from the storm, like streams of water in the desert and the shadow of a great rock in a thirsty land* (Is. 32:2).

Dying to Live

This is how we live as baptized children of God. In company with our brothers and sisters, under the cross. Daily dying and daily rising. Confessing our sin—dying the death we once died in Baptism by admitting the truth about our ugly sin. Receiving absolution from the mouth of our pastor for what it really is: the Word of forgiveness.

And there is life in that Word he speaks into our ears. It is the life of Jesus Christ.

6

Holy Supper: Feast of Life

This is my body given for you . . . This cup is the new covenant in my blood. (Luke 22:19, 20)

It was a long commute home that day, made longer by the emptiness of their hearts. Nobody felt much like talking—except for this stranger. Just who was he, anyway? How could he be so blissfully ignorant of their calamity? Woodenly, they filled him in on the whole sad story: from the early glory days of the movement to its bitter end, with their leader cut down in the prime of life. How would they ever survive without him? It was nearly sunset when they arrived home, and they invited the stranger in for dinner. At table, he picked up the bread and asked the blessing.

"Take, eat, this is my body," said Jesus.

Eyes to See

Some things are too important to be left to the eyes. Sometimes simple eyesight can't take in all there is to see. Take a baby, for example. The sight of an infant delights everyone, at least at first. But if that child is our own little son or daughter, you and I see much more in that baby than a stranger would see. Deeper realities lie beneath the surface. Other people might see just another baby, but when we see our very own flesh and blood, we see things you can't detect with simple lenses and retinas—things like love and affection.

Jesus explains that eyesight isn't always reliable when it comes to the things of God, either. *"The kingdom of God is not coming with signs to be observed; nor will they say, 'Lo, here it is!' or 'There!' for behold, the kingdom of God is in the midst of you"* (Luke 17:20–21, RSV). No one could see from external evidence that Jesus was God; yet when He stood in the middle of His disciples the kingdom of God had arrived. These things were not apparent to the naked eye.

They are known only by faith; the eyes of faith can see things regular eyes can't see. *Then he turned to his disciples and said privately, "Blessed are the eyes that see what you see. For I tell you that many prophets and kings wanted to see what you see but did not see it, and to hear what you hear but did not hear it"* (Luke 10:23–24).

It's no wonder Jesus was always teaching in parables. Ordinary language just wouldn't do justice to the things He had to say. And so He spoke in story and analogy to describe realities far deeper than human eyes could see. They were the hidden realities of the kingdom of God.

So it is in Christ's church today. The old "what you see is what you get" approach to reality simply won't do. If you and I are to grasp the bountiful riches of the gifts of God, ordinary eyesight and intellect won't work. For His gifts are wrapped in lowly packages: water, word, and meal. Yet behind these sacraments stands Jesus Himself and the power of His Holy Word. And there is life in His Word. The sacraments are tangible wrappings for that life-giving Word. This explains their historic nickname: "the visible word." For in the sacraments the invisible power of the Word of God lies wrapped in visible outer elements. Thus, in these sacraments we meet Jesus. Actually, in the sacraments Jesus meets us. And nowhere does He meet us more intimately than in that sacramental meal we call the Holy Supper.

Here history repeats itself. In His supper, Jesus dines with sinners for the forgiveness of their sins today, just as He did long ago.

Dining with Jesus

If there's one thing that really bothered the enemies of Jesus, it was that He was always hanging around the wrong crowd. If He were really a prophet of God, they reasoned, He'd be more interested in godly people. In their estimation, He spent too much time with the ungodly. Like Zacchaeus, for example.

St. Luke informs us that Zacchaeus lived in Jericho. He was a short man, a tax collector by profession. And that meant he was short on godliness, too. For tax collectors were agents of Rome, and they routinely took a cut for themselves from the taxes they collected. No wonder tax collectors were despised by the Jews. No doubt Zacchaeus, too, was despised as a traitor and a thief. He was not only a short man, he was short in spirit as well.

Since he couldn't see Jesus over the admiring throngs, Zacchaeus climbed a tree for a better view. You can imagine his surprise when Jesus stopped right in front of him with some shocking news: *"Zacchaeus, come down immediately. I must stay at your house today"* (Luke 19:5). Jesus didn't please the crowd with this request. They griped about it: *"He has gone to be the guest of a 'sinner'"* (19:7).

Jesus used to do this all the time. He often ate and drank with public sinners, conversing with them at table. It didn't earn Him the respect of the Pharisees and teachers of the Law, but Jesus didn't let their grumbling stop Him. *"It is not the healthy who need a doctor,"* He said, *"but the sick. I have not come to call the righteous, but sinners to repentance"* (Luke 5:31–32).

And that's what happened to Zacchaeus when Jesus sat at his table. A sinner was called to repentance that day. Before it was all over, Zacchaeus promised to give half his possessions to charity, with special provisions to pay back anyone he had cheated. *"Today salvation has come to this house,"* Jesus announced (19:9). And so it had. Salvation walked in the door when Jesus walked in. Salvation sat at table when Jesus sat down. And whenever Jesus spoke, salvation was speaking. And what Jesus used to say was always a variation on what He said at the home of that little man in Jericho: *"the Son of Man came to seek and to save what was lost"* (19:10). Wherever Jesus is, you see, there is forgiveness of sins. And where there is forgiveness of sins, there is life and salvation. That's what it's all about, this Christian faith.

That's what Christianity is, in fact. God's free gift of life and salvation in the presence of His Son, Jesus Christ. And we have the real presence of Jesus Christ in His Word and Sacrament.

Eating with Sinners

Jesus still uses the same mission strategy. Though risen and ascended to the Father's right hand in glory, Jesus Christ is present sacramentally today within His church. Though unseen to the naked eye, in His Holy Word and Sacrament Jesus still sits at table and teaches sinners of His love. What Jesus did in Jericho, He does even now in His church. And what happened there happens still today; people short on godliness but long on sin find forgiveness. And there is healing in that forgiveness. For wherever Jesus is present, there is life and salvation.

This is the essence of the sacred meal we call the Holy Supper of our Lord: the real presence of Jesus Christ with His church. In this meal, Jesus Christ dines with sinners. And, confessing their sin, sinners find forgiveness in Him. And life. And salvation.

Taken together, these three hidden realities: forgiveness, life, and salvation sum up the benefit of eating and drinking the Holy Supper of Jesus. Taken individually, each leads us into a different biblical dimension of this wonderful meal. Please join me on a brief excursion down each path. The journey leads us first into the past, where we examine a meal eaten under cover of darkness, in haste and deadly fear. Then we consider the life Jesus Christ dispenses every time we eat His holy meal. Finally we venture into the very courts of heaven, for in Christ's supper we anticipate an eternal, joyous feast, where there is no night, and death has passed away.

FEAST OF FORGIVENESS

The Paschal Meal

The first thing to know about the Sacrament of the Altar, as it is sometimes called, is that it's a meal. The Lord's Supper, we call it. And so it is. For in this supper, Jesus Christ Himself is not only the host but the main course as well:

> For I received from the Lord what I also passed on to you: The Lord Jesus, on the night he was betrayed, took bread, and when he had given thanks, he broke it and said, "This is my body, which is for you; do this in remembrance of me." In the same way, after supper he took the cup, saying, "This cup is the new covenant in my blood; do this, whenever you drink it, in remembrance of me." (1 Cor. 11:23–25)

What sort of meal is this, in which believers are invited to dine on Christ's body and blood? Why is this body "for you?" What does Jesus mean by "the new covenant in my blood?" And how about eating and drinking "in remembrance of me"? These questions about the Lord's Supper lead us to the Old Testament supper of ancient Israel: the Passover, or Pascha, as God's people called it.

In the Shadow of Death

The origins of Passover are found in Exodus 12, where we find Israel preparing for an emergency trip. For 430 years Israel had lived in exile in Egypt. By the end that exile had turned into bitter slavery and oppression under the Pharaoh. But God had plans to deliver His people through His servant Moses.

> "Moreover, I have heard the groaning of the Israelites, whom the Egyptians are enslaving, and I have remembered my covenant. "Therefore, say to the Israelites: 'I am the LORD, and I will bring you out from under the yoke of the Egyptians. I will free you from being slaves to them, and I will redeem you with an outstretched arm and with mighty acts of judgment. I will take you as my own people, and I will be your God. Then you will know that I am the LORD your God, who brought you out from under the yoke of the Egyptians. And I will bring you to the land I swore with uplifted hand to give to Abraham, to Isaac and to Jacob. I will give it to you as a possession. I am the LORD.' " (Ex. 6:5–8)

We've already seen how God won a decisive victory over Pharaoh and his army in the drowning at the Red Sea, a prototype of Christian Baptism. The origins of Passover—and thus the roots of the Lord's Supper—are found in the negotiations between Moses and Pharaoh over the release of his Hebrew slaves.

Time and again Pharaoh promised to let God's people go and release them for a journey back to their homeland. But each time he changed his mind. Finally, God decided to play hardball with Pharaoh. All first-born people or animals in the whole land of Egypt would die. Yet in His mercy, God provided a way of escape for the Israelites through the death of a sacrificial lamb:

> "The animals you choose must be year-old males without defect, and you may take them from the sheep or the goats. Take care of them until the fourteenth day of the month, when all the people of the community of Israel must slaughter them at twilight. Then they are to take some of the blood and put it on the sides and tops of the doorframes of the houses where they eat

the lambs. That same night they are to eat the meat roasted over the fire, along with bitter herbs, and bread made without yeast. Do not eat the meat raw or cooked in water, but roast it over the fire—head, legs and inner parts. Do not leave any of it till morning; if some is left till morning, you must burn it. This is how you are to eat it: with your cloak tucked into your belt, your sandals on your feet and your staff in your hand. Eat it in haste; it is the Lord's Passover. On that same night I will pass through Egypt and strike down every firstborn—both men and animals—and I will bring judgment on all the gods of Egypt. I am the LORD. (Exodus 12:5–12)

Here are the roots of the Lord's Supper. In this most remarkable meal, the main course was the antidote to certain death. For God not only said what He meant, He meant what He said. There would be retribution for the stubborn rebellion of Pharaoh. There were to be no exceptions. Death would be exacted from every household—except where the blood of a lamb marked the doorway. In those homes a death had already occurred. The lamb—the Pascha, or "Passover"—had already given up its life, and so the avenging angel would pass over that house on his deadly journey through Egypt.

Every blood-smeared door was a sign both to the inhabitants of that house and to God. By this sign God pledged His deliverance to His people, and by the same sign those who lived within that house found comfort and solace in the very face of death. This was not "just pretend." The wages of sin is death, and that awful night God dealt out the just penalty for sin. Of all the houses without a sacrificial lamb, not a single one remained untouched by death. *There was loud wailing in Egypt,* we read (12:30). We can certainly understand why. For death was on the prowl that night. And fear was in the air.

There was fear in the blood-marked homes of the Hebrews, too. But it was a holy fear, tinged with joy. They dined on roasted lamb, and not simply for nourishment. It was their participation—their communion—in the sign of God's deliverance for them. The very lamb which had delivered them from death by the shedding of its blood was also the main course in this meal. In this supper there was life in the face of death. Here was a deliverance they could sink their teeth into. In the very shadow of death, God was delivering

His people. That very night the Lord delivered them from death and led them out of bondage. This was a night to be remembered.

A Memorial Meal

We've all seen great memorials constructed to recall key events in the history of a nation or to commemorate important people. If you've ever been to Washington, D.C., perhaps you've been moved by the overwhelming power of the Lincoln Monument or the eloquent simplicity of the Vietnam War Memorial. But no blocks of stone were erected to observe the deliverance of Israel from Egypt. Instead, God prescribed an annual Passover.

> "You shall observe this rite as an ordinance for you and for your sons for ever. And when you come to the land which the LORD will give you, as He has promised, you shall keep this service. And when your children say to you, 'What do you mean by this service?' you shall say, 'It is the sacrifice of the LORD's passover, for He passed over the houses of the people of Israel in Egypt, when He slew the Egyptians but spared our houses.'" And the people bowed their heads and worshiped. (Ex. 12:24–27 RSV)

In all of history, there was only one night when God delivered His people Israel from death and bondage in Egypt. But there were to be repeated Passovers. Annually the same menu would be served. Annually the same Psalms would be sung. Annually the same prayers would be prayed. It was a "rite," a ritual which recalled perpetually everything God had done for Israel. But more than that, it had contemporary application. No matter how many generations went by, every year the youngest child asked, "What is the meaning of this service?" And every year parents would respond in the present tense. They were not just recalling a past event, they were sharing in it: "This is the night of our deliverance," they said. "This is the night the Lord slew the Egyptians but spared our houses."

In Remembrance of Jesus

Do this, whenever you drink it, said Jesus the night of His betrayal, *in remembrance of me.* And we, like Israelite children

97

before us, ask: "What is the meaning of this service?" Is it simply kneeling at the Communion rail and thinking back about the deliverance God won for us at Calvary? Is it digging into our memory for an event out of past? Is it remembering Jesus, as we would reminisce about a departed loved one? What, really, is the meaning of the Communion rite?

Here Jesus helps us out. *Take and eat; this is my body,* He says of the Communion bread. And regarding the Communion wine, He says: *Drink of it, all of you. For this is My blood of the last will and testament, which is being poured out for many for the forgiveness of sins* (Matt. 26:26–28 NET). This is no mere exercise in memory recall. This is the real thing. This eating and drinking is the meal of our deliverance.

As it was in the Passover, so it is in the Holy Supper. Time and space are transcended. Israel was delivered from bondage in Egypt only once; and yet the annual Passover was its repeated participation in that climactic deliverance. So too, Jesus gave His body and shed His blood only once on the cross. And yet in His holy meal He distributes that very same body and blood again and again for us Christians to eat and to drink. *Do this,* invites Jesus, *in remembrance of me* (1 Cor. 11:24).

In remembrance of me cuts in two directions. In this sacramental eating and drinking we remember Jesus, and He also remembers us. At the center of this remembering is the very body and blood once given for the forgiveness of sins. The "remembrance" in this meal is far more than just a memory exercise!

For this sacred meal is a living memorial in two distinct and yet inseparable ways. In this supper we continually recall our redemption. It is the sign of our deliverance from certain death as we eat the body of the true Lamb of God who takes away our sins. Yet in this holy meal God the Father also remembers the new testament in the blood of His Son, the sign and seal of His redeeming love. This testament stands forever sure, founded on the incarnate body and blood of the Son of God. In His instructions, Jesus Christ Himself points out for His church the benefit of this eating and drinking: *given and shed for you for the forgiveness of sins.*

Proclaiming His Death

In this supper Jesus preaches a powerful sermon for us. Each time we eat and drink His body and blood once given and shed we participate in all the benefits He earned for us on His cross. Here the forgiveness of sins is personally applied. Not only did Jesus die for the sins of all the world, but in this sacred meal through His called servants He hands us the actual body and blood He once gave and says, *for you for the forgiveness of sins.*

This is powerful public testimony. It is personal testimony, direct from God, addressed personally to us. This Sacrament offers, gives, and seals the same forgiveness as a Gospel sermon. The difference is that in the eating and drinking it's applied to us individually and personally: *for you for the remission of sins.* And sometimes a personal address makes all the difference in the world. Think for a minute which kind of mail you prefer; a third-class flyer addressed to "occupant" or a first-class letter with your name on it?

Our living Lord hasn't left anything to chance. Because we are inclined to doubt the forgiveness of our sins, Jesus presents us with the tangible results of His death on our behalf. Just as a canceled check is evidence of purchase, so His body once broken and His blood once shed is the sign of sins forgiven. Under the bread and wine of His Holy Supper, Jesus Christ hands us the sign of our deliverance from sin and death. Take eat, He says, . . . *my body given for you. . . . the new covenant in my blood, which is poured out for many for the forgiveness of sins (Luke 22:19; Matt. 26:28).* Here there is encouragement for faith. Here there is reason to rejoice. For this is the meal of our deliverance in the forgiveness of our sins.

In turn, every communicant gives powerful public testimony in the eating and drinking of this Holy Supper. Our testimony in this meal is not just before people at the Communion rail, but before angels and archangels and all the company of heaven as well: *For whenever you eat this bread and drink this cup, you proclaim the Lord's death until he comes* (1 Cor. 11:26).

One Common Enemy

It's interesting that the Old Testament models for Baptism and the Lord's Supper both have a common origin in Israel's deliverance from bondage in Egypt. The Red Sea victory and the Passover rescue were directed against the same enemy, Pharaoh. So also the sacraments of Holy Baptism and Communion are signs and seals of Christ's victory over one ancient foe, the devil. In these outward signs He offers hidden realities for our hearts to believe. And believing, we rejoice. For in the victory over Satan there is also victory over the fallen world and our own sinful nature.

Just as both sacraments are directed against the same powerful enemy, so they also have one crucial benefit: the forgiveness of sins. Peter instructed the crowd who heard him on Pentecost Day: *Repent and be baptized, every one of you, in the name of Jesus Christ for the forgiveness of your sins. And you will receive the gift of the Holy Spirit* (Acts 2:38). In His Holy Supper Jesus specifies His blood as poured out *for the forgiveness of sins.* (Matt. 26:28).

A Blood Payment

Without the shedding of blood, there is no forgiveness, the letter to the Hebrews reminds us (9:22). To modern ears, such language seems crude. Despite the violence in our culture, we generally think we're quite sophisticated and refined. And so we find this connection between the shedding of blood and the forgiveness of sins puzzling, if not downright revolting.

Actually, there is something revolting here. Sin is revolting; it involves a pact with death and the devil. In the first chapter of this book I described the ugly reality of our bondage to sin. Though that bondage takes a different shape for each of us, it's always spelled the same way: D-E-A-T-H. That's the revolting reality of sin. Sin spells certain death for us today, just as it did for Adam and Eve: *when you eat of it you will surely die* (Gen. 2:17).

There is only one way for death to die; only one way death's cosmic spell can be broken—if God Himself pays the penalty. And that's precisely what He did when He sent His sinless Son to bear all the sins of all the world in His own body. By His death, Jesus Christ redeemed the world; He broke the back of death and the grave.

But all through the Old Testament, God was preparing the way for that final cosmic victory. In Israel's daily liturgy, God vividly reminded His people that sin carried the death penalty. Day after day animals were led to the slaughter in the holy precincts of the temple. Day after day the smoke of the altar of burnt offering made its menacing way to the sky, with the stench of burning flesh underscoring the horrid consequences of sin. Day after day the blood of sacrificial animals ran vividly to the floor. The shedding of that blood indicated the full extent of the sacrificial payment: *For the life of a creature is in the blood, and I have given it to you to make atonement for yourselves on the altar; it is the blood that makes atonement for one's life* (Lev. 17:11).

The Blood of the New Testament

Still, the blood of animals was not adequate payment. It could cleanse from sin outwardly, but not within. The stranglehold of death remained in force under the Old Covenant. God promised a New Covenant, not like the first. And so it was that God's people looked to the future for redemption. Every lamb slaughtered in the temple anticipated the real Lamb to come, whose blood would be shed on the cross as the final atonement.

> The blood of goats and bulls and the ashes of a heifer sprinkled on those who are ceremonially unclean sanctify them so that they are outwardly clean. How much more, then, will the blood of Christ, who through the eternal Spirit offered himself unblemished to God, cleanse our consciences from acts that lead to death, so that we may serve the living God! For this reason Christ is the mediator of a new covenant, that those who are called may receive the promised eternal inheritance—now that he has died as a ransom to set them free from the sins committed under the first covenant. (Heb. 9:13–15)

As it was under the first covenant, so it is in the new covenant. Only better. In fact, we often refer to the new covenant as the New Testament, emphasizing the inheritance bestowed on us by our gracious God. Sacrificial lambs could remove external uncleanness; but the true Lamb cleansed our hearts from sin by His sacrifice. Israel's annual pasch, or passover lamb, was a meal of remem-

101

brance. It recalled a deliverance from bondage under the Old Covenant in Egypt; but the true Lamb continually presents His church with the New Testament in His blood, by which He breaks the bonds of sin and death.

There is forgiveness in that blood. For it is the blood of God.

FEAST OF LIFE

One Holy Food

The church is the New Testament people of God. Like Israel in the Old Testament, the church is on a journey. She is on her way to the eternal promised land in heaven. And like Israel, the church wanders in a wilderness—the wilderness of this world. Dangers lurk on every side. The devil, the world, and our own sinful nature strive to do us in. We need protection, but we also need food. We need the bread of heaven, or we will die in this world.

Remembering the bounty of Egypt, the people of Israel grumbled against Moses and Aaron in the wilderness: *you have brought us out into this desert to starve this entire assembly to death. Then the Lord said to Moses: "I will rain down bread from heaven for you"* (Ex. 16:3–4). And so it was that God fed His people with manna, the bread from heaven.

You and I can understand those people. For, like Israel, we sometimes long for the comfort and security of slavery. They longed for the captivity of Egypt; we long for the captivity of sin. We curse the jails we've built for ourselves, but we also find them strangely comforting. There's a perverse security to our bondage, for like all addicts we begin to believe a lie. We imagine we need our sins to survive. Sometimes we get to the point where we actually feed on alternate fits of rage and remorse. To minds so twisted by sin, forgiveness seems oddly threatening. And so like the Israelites in the wilderness, we sometimes prefer death in slavery to life in freedom. We begin to think that death as slaves to sin is preferable to a life of freedom as the children of God.

But our God is just as merciful and patient with us as He was with ancient Israel. Though they craved the food of slavery, God fed them instead with the bread of sonship. As it was then, so it is now. Just as God fed His Old Testament people with bread from heaven along their wilderness journey, so He feeds His New Testament church on our trek toward home. And the food He gives us is exactly the same food He gave them: *They all ate the same spiritual food and drank the same spiritual drink; for they drank from the spiritual rock that accompanied them, and that rock was Christ* (1 Cor. 10:3–4).

Once Israel collected manna from the ground and drank from a water-giving rock in the wilderness. You and I eat and drink the Holy Supper of our Lord. But our strength and nourishment is one and the same: the Lord Jesus Christ. He is the Living Bread from heaven. Whoever eats this bread lives forever.

Bread in the Wilderness

The Jews of Capernaum were looking for a sign. They wanted to know if Jesus was really sent by God the Father. They offered a test: Moses had supplied their ancestors with bread from heaven. How about Jesus providing a continuous supply of the miraculous food He gave on the shores of Galilee? It sounded like a good deal to them.

Jesus had another idea:

> I tell you the truth, it is not Moses who has given you the bread from heaven, but it is my Father who gives you the true bread from heaven. For the bread of God is he who comes down from heaven and gives life to the world. (John 6:32–33)

You can read the sixth chapter of John for yourself. It's a remarkable discourse from Jesus on His body and blood as the true bread from God. Though some of it is hard to grasp, what's plain to see is His call for faith: *I tell you the truth, he who believes has everlasting life* (6:47). "Spiritual eating and drinking," some have called this. And they're absolutely right; this is crucial. For without faith, physical eating and drinking of the Holy Supper has no spiritual benefit.

For the Life of the World

But there's more. The heavenly gifts of God are given *in* tangible wrappings. Spiritual eating and drinking are joined *with* physical eating and drinking. The bread of heaven is given *under* earthly bread. Admittedly, this is no ordinary eating and drinking. But then, the Holy Supper is no ordinary meal. It is the supper of our Lord.

The trouble with the manna Israel ate in the wilderness, explained Jesus, is that the Israelites died after all. There is another kind of bread from heaven, however, which is both edible and death-defying: *I am the living bread that came down from heaven. If anyone eats of this bread, he will live forever. This bread is my flesh, which I will give for the life of the world* (6:51).

In Him was life, wrote St. John, *and that life was the light of men* (1:4). And, you'll recall from chapter 2, that's exactly who Jesus was and is: the incarnate Son of God, the life of the world. Embodied life. Life in person in a world full of death. This life-giving flesh of His would be the very offering given for the life of the world, Jesus explained. And those who heard Him were willing to listen. But when He went on, it became a bit much to stomach:

> I tell you the truth, unless you eat the flesh of the Son of Man and drink his blood, you have no life in you. Whoever eats my flesh and drinks my blood has eternal life, and I will raise him up at the last day. For my flesh is real food and my blood is real drink. Whoever eats my flesh and drinks my blood remains in me, and I in him. Just as the living Father sent me and I live because of the Father, so the one who feeds on me will live because of me. This is the bread that came down from heaven. Your forefathers ate manna and died, but he who feeds on this bread will live forever. (6:53–58)

This is a hard teaching, they replied. *Who can accept it?* (6:60). You and I would agree. It's hard to grasp how Jesus can feed us with His actual body and blood once given and shed for the life of the world. These things are hard to listen to, much less believe. But then, that's the point. You have to have ears to hear, said Jesus. And to hear the things Jesus teaches us, one must have the ears He gives. Some things can't be seen with ordinary eyes, and some things can't be heard with ordinary ears.

But blessed are the eyes that see and the ears that hear; the eyes and ears of faith. For in the Holy Supper these hidden realities are present and distributed at our altars every Lord's Day: the very body and blood of Christ—heavenly food for the earthly people of God.

The flesh of Jesus is the bread of God come down from heaven to give life to the world. That bread sustains us in this world on our wilderness journey toward our heavenly home.

The Holy Supper of our Lord is not a symbolic meal. When we eat this bread and drink this cup we're not playing "let's pretend." For in, with, and under the bread and wine of this Sacrament Jesus gives us His true body and true blood. His flesh is real food, and His blood is real drink.

And there is life in that flesh and blood, for it is the flesh and blood of God.

FEAST OF SALVATION

The Wedding Feast to Come

Past, present, and future—these three dimensions are all part of Christ's Holy Supper. Like Israel of old, we commemorate in our eating and drinking a past event: God's decisive victory at the cross, which means the forgiveness of our sins. And in this Holy Supper there is the present reality of the presence of Jesus Christ Himself, who in the eating and drinking nourishes us with His life-giving body and blood. But the supper also has a future aspect. It looks forward to heaven itself, thereby anticipating the culmination of our salvation in an eternal feast to come.

We live in an age with a fixation on the "now." Politicians may come up with ideas on lowering the national debt, for example, but few of us are willing to sacrifice current income for the sake of the future. Businesses may have strategies for growth and people may make retirement plans, but by and large the overpowering realities of the present take precedent over shadowy images of the future. We are a people locked in the tyranny of the now. And—let's face it—when all is said and done, the now isn't always that pleasant. The Holy Supper of our Lord, however, reminds us that there is a future for the people of God; a glorious future.

The night of His betrayal, Jesus pointed His disciples to the future:

> And he said to them, "I have eagerly desired to eat this Passover with you before I suffer. For I tell you, I will not eat it again until it finds fulfillment in the kingdom of God." After taking

the cup, he gave thanks and said, "Take this and divide it among you. For I tell you I will not drink again of the fruit of the vine until the kingdom of God comes." (Luke 22:15–18)

Three days later He fulfilled His promise. Sitting at table with His Emmaus disciples, He took bread, blessed and broke it and gave it to them. Though St. Luke doesn't say so explicitly, it seems from the context that this supper on Easter evening was the Lord's Supper. The disciples, Luke informs us, hurried back to Jerusalem and breathlessly informed the Eleven that the reports were in fact true; Jesus had risen from the dead. *Then they told what had happened on the road, and how he was known to them in the breaking of the bread.* (Luke 24:35 RSV). "The breaking of the bread," a phrase used repeatedly in the book of Acts, was an early designation for the Sacrament of the Altar.

It's a remarkable narrative, and all the more remarkable when we consider its significance for us. First we have Jesus talking about a future paschal eating and drinking in the kingdom of God, and then three days later we find Jesus eating and drinking the same meal with His disciples. What happened during those intervening three days? Good Friday and Easter. The Cross and the Resurrection. The implications are clear. In His dying and rising, Jesus Christ inaugurated the fullness of the kingdom of God. All that God had promised His people from the beginning found its fulfillment in Christ's atoning sacrifice. His Easter day was the first day of the new creation. God's kingdom had come at last.

Christ's Holy Supper is essentially a banquet for the forgiveness of sins. Here we eat and drink in remembrance of past deliverance. But this is no mere memorial meal, for the menu is the very body given and the very blood shed for the life of the world. Each time we eat and drink there is the present reality of sins forgiven and life restored. In her earthly eating and drinking the church celebrates a royal feast. It is the celebration of her heavenly Bridegroom and anticipation of the wedding feast to come. "Where there is forgiveness of sins," Luther reminds us, "there is also life and salvation." And so there is. It is the life and salvation of God, which finds its culmination in the heavenly feast.

Dining with God

Thanks to the fast-food industry and the breakneck pace of modern life, the whole concept of a "feast to come" seems to have lost something. To most of us, it may mean nothing more than a large meal—a grand buffet table, for instance, overflowing with an abundance of food.

To the ancients, however, a feast was not simply a time to eat a lot of food; it was a time of celebration and unity. We've already seen how some people were put off by Jesus when He sat and dined publicly with notorious sinners. By eating with them, He showed solidarity with them. More important, Jesus called sinners to repentance and salvation in these fellowship meals. His eating and drinking with sinners was a vivid sign of God's peace in this world.

Because He had come to take away the sins of the world, Jesus was able to receive sinners and eat with them. And His presence with sinners changed their lives. The meal at the house of Zacchaeus is a case in point. The salvation of Zacchaeus was not in his penitent vow to repay what he had taken by fraud. Jesus Himself was the salvation of Zacchaeus; his change of heart flowed from his faith in Jesus. As it was in Jericho, so it is among us. Wherever Jesus eats and drinks with sinners, salvation arrives in that place, and hearts are repeatedly turned to repentance and faith.

A Covenantal Meal

Zacchaeus' house in Jericho was not the first place sinners had dined in the presence of God. A long time before that a remarkable meal had taken place on Mount Sinai, where God revealed His presence to Israel in a most extraordinary way.

> Then Moses led the people out of the camp to meet with God, and they stood at the foot of the mountain. Mount Sinai was covered with smoke, because the Lord descended on it in fire. The smoke billowed up from it like smoke from a furnace, the whole mountain trembled violently, and the sound of the trumpet grew louder and louder. (Ex. 19:17–19)

In no uncertain terms, God warned Moses of the disastrous impact of His holy presence for sinful mankind: *"Go down and warn the people so they do not force their way through to see the LORD and many of them perish. Even the priests, who approach the LORD, must consecrate themselves, or the LORD will break out against them"* (19:21–22). Like fire and water, the sacred presence of God does not mix with the foul pollution of sin. In the presence of the holy God, one must be holy. For sin is destroyed in the presence of holiness. If it were not for the redeeming blood of Christ, sinners could not approach God without being destroyed. By His blood sinners are cleansed and made holy.

Yet even at Sinai, amid earthquake and fire and the loud trumpet blast of God's holy presence, there was peace for sinners. It was a peace established at God's initiative by means of a sacred covenant. He promised to be their God, and they promised to be His people. God's covenant with Israel was His peace treaty with His rebellious children.

And there was cleansing blood at Sinai, though it was only a preview of the real thing. Acting on God's instructions, Moses took the blood of sacrificial oxen and divided it into two portions. Half of it he reserved in bowls and half of it He threw against the altar of God. *Then he took the Book of the Covenant and read it to the people. They responded, "We will do everything the LORD has said; we will obey." Moses then took the blood, sprinkled it on the people and said, "This is the blood of the covenant that the LORD has made with you in accordance with all these words"* (24:7–8). And so God's treaty with His people was signed, sealed, and delivered in blood.

Even in our culture today it's still common to seal major business deals or international agreements with a celebratory feast. So also at Sinai.

> Moses and Aaron, Nadab and Abihu, and the seventy elders of Israel went up and saw the God of Israel. Under his feet was something like a pavement made of sapphire, clear as the sky itself. But God did not raise his hand against these leaders of the Israelites; they saw God, and they ate and drank. (24:9–11)

The contrast is striking. Prior to the covenant God sternly warned the leaders of His people against the disastrous effect of His holy presence on sinners. Once His covenant had been put into effect, however, sinners who were cleansed could eat and drink in His presence without fear. Atonement had been made. His wrath had broken out against the sacrificial animals instead of the sinners, you see. This animal blood was the blood of God's covenant. But it was only a shadow of things to come, for *it is impossible for the blood of bulls and goats to take away sins* (Heb. 10:4).

The real sacrificial blood came some 14 centuries later. On the night He was betrayed, Jesus Christ, the true Lamb of Israel, about to shed His blood for the salvation of the whole world, took the Passover cup and said to His disciples: "Take, drink, this is the new testament in my blood." These words recalled the covenant at Sinai established in animal blood. But this covenant is now passé—there is a "new testament" in the blood of God's own Son. Sinai is the picture; Calvary is the reality. At Sinai the blood of oxen was first offered on God's altar and then sprinkled on His people. At Calvary the Son of God offered His holy, precious blood once on the cross and now in His Holy Supper continually distributes that blood together with His body for us Christians to eat and to drink.

Thus in the Holy Supper a New Testament is repeatedly affirmed. Like the Old Covenant, it is a testament of blood; yet signed, sealed, and delivered, not in animal blood, but in the blood of God. Unlike the Old Covenant, this New Testament establishes the reality of the forgiveness of sins and peace with God. Made holy in the blood of Jesus Christ, we come boldly before our holy God.

Once Moses and Aaron, Nadab and Abihu, and the 70 Israelite elders dined in the presence of God on the slopes of Sinai; but it was a meal only for the elite. The rest of the people of Israel still had to keep their distance. The Lord's Supper has a bigger guest list; for Jesus Christ has erased the penalty of our sin by His perfect obedience, suffering, and death. The gates of heaven stand open, thanks to Him.

In the presence of the holy God, you and I must be holy. And that's just it; by faith in Christ we are holy. Now all who trust in Him may safely eat and drink in the presence of God in perfect peace. And so those who dined on the slopes of Sinai have nothing over us. For whenever we eat and drink the body and blood of our Lord, we're eating and drinking in the very presence of God. That's a present reality in this Sacrament.

Heaven on Earth

Yet in this holy meal, as I mentioned earlier, there is also a future dimension. For the Holy Supper is a foretaste of something greater to come. In this sacred meal we consume with our mortal bodies the medicine of the immortal life which is in Jesus Christ, the Living Bread come down from heaven. Here in this world we see the presence of God only dimly by faith. But there in heaven's glory we shall see God face to face and eat and drink in His presence forevermore.

That eternal banquet is the marriage supper of the Lamb, Scripture informs us. And in that future feast there shall be eternal nuptial joy. For it is the marriage supper of the royal Son of God and His holy bride, the church. That will be a wedding day to end all wedding days!

> Let us rejoice and be glad and give him glory! For the wedding of the Lamb has come, and his bride has made herself ready. (Rev. 19:7)
>
> I saw the Holy City, the new Jerusalem, coming down out of heaven from God, prepared as a bride beautifully dressed for her husband. And I heard a loud voice from the throne saying, "Now the dwelling of God is with men, and he will live with them. They will be his people, and God himself will be with them and be their God. He will wipe every tear from their eyes. There will be no more death or mourning or crying or pain, for the old order of things has passed away." (Rev. 21:2–4)

A Table before Me

Here in the valley of the shadow of death our Good Shepherd not only leads us beside the still waters of His grace and into the green pastures of His love, He also prepares a table before us. In the supper He sets before us in this world we have a banquet of His love for the world to come. There is solace and peace in this meal set before us openly in the presence of all our enemies, for it is the perpetual sign of His redeeming love.

"Lift up your hearts," the ancient liturgy calls out to all Christ's own. "We lift them up unto the Lord," the church responds in every age. And well she might. For in this holy meal the heavenly bridegroom invites His earthly bride to leave behind the things of earth and ponder the eternal nuptial joys to come. And so through the church, together with angels and archangels and all the company of heaven, the song goes on forever new:

"Worthy is the Lamb, who was slain, to receive power and wealth and wisdom and strength and honor and glory and praise!" (Rev. 5:12)

From Christ's own body blood and water once flowed out in His death. Now He is risen from the dead, never to die again. Ascended to the Father's right hand, He lives and reigns to all eternity. All the mighty powers and all the majestic authorities of the universe are subject to Him; they are as footstools for His feet.

And God placed all things under his feet and appointed him to be head over everything for the church, which is his body, the fullness of him who fills everything in every way. (Eph. 1:22–23)

And yet this Lord who rules in exalted glory is the Crucified One. Even now from His own glorified body He sends forth forgiveness, life, and salvation in a never-ending stream. Christ, the heavenly Bridegroom, feeds His beloved with His very body broken and blood once shed. It is a banquet of love—a veritable feast of salvation.

Here is a feast to be remembered. Though dying in this world, we have life in this feast. For here we dine on the body and blood of Christ. And in Him we have life never-ending.

PART 3

The Liturgical Shape of the Christian Life

7

Divine Service: Liturgical Life Together

The LORD will cause His glorious voice to be heard.(Is. 30:30 NKJV)

The old gang just wouldn't be the same anymore. The tenants always used to get together with the landlord's son, but now he was going back to join his father. The bottom seemed to drop out of their life. They stared hopelessly at each other. How would they ever manage things by themselves?

"Where two or more are gathered in my name," said Jesus, "there am I in their midst."

A Continuing Pilgrimage

You and I have covered a lot of terrain by now. Together we've explored the horrifying depths of the human heart, locked in the bondage of sin and death. And we have surveyed the heights of God's love and life, taking careful note of both its foundation and its focus. We've investigated the incarnational foundation of the Christian life; rooted solidly in the body and blood of Jesus Christ, within which all the fullness of God was pleased to dwell. And we have examined the sacramental focus of the Christian life; in His Holy Word and Sacrament God continues to lavish on His people the forgiveness, life, and salvation earned by His Son. So far, so good. Since we've covered the foundation and focus of the Christian life, I suppose I could stop right here.

But I won't. For our journey isn't over yet. I would be letting you down if I didn't let you in on a little secret: the Christian life has more than a foundation and a focus, it has a certain shape as well. And that shape is a liturgical shape. Now when I bring up the liturgy, some of you might be tempted to put this book down. But

I hope you won't, for we still have a lot of important ground to cover on this pilgrimage of ours.

Don't worry. This section isn't going to be all about "smells and bells": candles and chanting and vestments and incense and things like that. There are plenty of other books about those things, and I commend them for your consideration. Likewise, there are lots of good books on the structure of the liturgy, its scriptural background, and its meaning for contemporary Christians. No sense in duplicating those materials here; you can read them for yourself.

What I would like to explore with you in these last three chapters is how the Christian life is lived as one great liturgy, or divine service. It includes God's service to us and our service to Him, but first and last and always it is God's action. Everything we do in the Christian life is therefore liturgical from beginning to end—including public worship, which is liturgical life together; our private prayers and meditation, which is liturgical life alone; and the service we perform in our vocation, which is liturgical life in the world.

In this chapter we take a closer look at our liturgical life together in community.

God's Action or Ours?

As we approach the end of the 20th century, Christians of many different denominational stripes are vigorously debating just what's supposed to be going on in the church's worship. This is not simply another instance of traditionalists aligned against the avant-garde. True, on the surface the question seems to be the proper balance between traditional style and contemporary style in worship forms. But a deeper, perhaps unprecedented issue lies at the heart of the matter: JUST WHAT IS WORSHIP IN THE FIRST PLACE?

We'll never resolve issues revolving around the *how* of public worship until we tackle the *what* of public worship. Is the weekly gathering of Christians just another public assembly of like-minded people—such as a meeting of corporate sales reps, for instance? Or is the worshiping congregation itself God's own creation, called into being by God Himself? The way you answer that question has profound implications for determining how worship is conducted.

116

More important, it has profound implications for how you and I live as Christians in this world.

Pathology and Cure

If, for example, sin is merely a moral blemish on an otherwise impeccable human character, then Christian assemblies can be devoted to moral improvement, using emotive and psychological tools of the trade. Then the worship service is essentially one big self-help group, and the pastor is a large-group therapist.

If on the other hand, sin actually means bondage and death—as I've suggested in the first chapter—then the worshiping congregation takes on an entirely different character. It is an island of life on an ocean of death. It is God's hospital for the terminally ill. And that's what the church truly is: God's hospital—the fellowship in which the Holy Trinity dispenses the medicine of heaven for this dying world. And the arena of public worship is the surgical suite, where the divine Surgeon goes to work with the scalpel of His Holy Word and Sacrament, cutting out the cancer of sin and death.

Remember, there's no way to life except through death. This is the route engraved in the cosmos itself, for it is inscribed on the very heart of our Creator: *"See now that I, even I, am He, and there is no god beside Me; I kill and I make alive; I wound and I heal; and there is none that can deliver out of My hand"* (Deut. 32:39 RSV). As it was in the beginning, so it is now and ever will be: God is always bringing life out of death. He is by definition a life-giver, but the only way He can heal is to wound. And the only way He can make alive is to kill.

We've already seen how God kills in order to bestow life through Holy Baptism; in that bath of life each believer is plunged into death. We were first buried in that water with Jesus Christ into His death and then raised with Him to live His new life.

When we step into church for public worship each week we step into the presence of God the life-giver. There the sin which clings so closely to us shows up for what it really is: what appeared to be the bright garments of personal fulfillment are shown to be the tattered rags of rebellion—dangerous attire in the presence of the

117

living God. Yet God in His mercy provides proper apparel; sinners are stripped of their sin and clothed in Christ's righteousness.

God the life-giver embraces the sinner with His love in the divine service. That embrace spells the death of sin and the renewal of the new man in Christ. The hymns, the prayers, the readings, and the timeless songs of the ancient liturgy engulf the sinner in the Word of God. And so history is repeated. Once again sin drowns and dies and the new man emerges to live before God in righteousness and purity.

The life-giving God is present in His church to carry on week in and week out what He initiated once for all at the cross and for every believer personally in Holy Baptism. In the surgical suite of public worship He operates on terminally ill sinners; He brings life out of death.

His surgical instruments of healing are His Holy Word and Sacrament.

A Christian Mantra?

You might be getting tired of hearing me repeat that handy little phrase: Word and Sacrament. The fact is, it does get tossed around a lot in the church, and in some circles it's become something of a mantra; words with more feeling than content. But let me assure you, there is nothing mantralike about these words. For behind God's Word and Sacrament stands the very power and authority of God, rooted solidly in the incarnate flesh of His Son. And there is life in that flesh, for it is the flesh of God.

The truth is that the written and oral Word of God is the living power of the living God. At bottom, the Word of God is Jesus Christ Himself, the Word made flesh. There is only one Word, but more than one sacrament. God is surprisingly rich in His grace. He gives the comfort and peace of the forgiveness of our sins in more than one way. Yet there is only one source of life in this dying world. The Word and the Sacraments throb with life; the life which first was pleased to take up residence in His incarnate flesh resides for us in these lowly channels of washing, word, and meal. You cannot understand the sacraments apart from the Word of God, nor can you grasp the power of the Word until you see it sacramentally. One reality stands behind both: the Son of God made flesh. And so whether it's the oral word of the Gospel or the tangible word of the sacraments, it's all the same word: the Word of the Father made flesh for us and for our salvation.

The words I have spoken to you, said Jesus, *are spirit and they are life* (John 6:63). *As the living Father sent Me, and I live because of the Father, so he who eats Me will live because of Me* (6:57 RSV). Jesus Christ is embodied life. And so, whether oral or tangible, the word of His gospel is always the Word of the Son of God, which is by definition also the Word of the Father and of the Spirit. Therefore the word of the Gospel in either spoken or sacramental form always means the same thing for us Christians when we gather for public worship: forgiveness, life, and salvation—God's forgiveness, God's life, God's salvation here and now in this dying world in the midst of His congregation.

Devoted to the Fellowship

No wonder, then, that from the very beginning the Christian church has always centered its life around God's Holy Word and Sacrament. Take the first Christian congregation in Jerusalem, for example. We read that on Pentecost Day 3,000 believed and were baptized. And then: *they devoted themselves to the apostles' teaching and fellowship, to the breaking of bread and the prayers* (Acts 2:42 RSV). A friend of mine points out that the Greek word for "they devoted themselves" could better be rendered "they persisted obstinately." Why were they so devoted; why did they persist so obstinately in these things?

When we take this sentence apart phrase by phrase we see why. What else was the "apostles' teaching" than the oral word of the Gospel conveyed to them by Jesus Himself before His ascension and safeguarded by operation of the Holy Spirit? What else was the "breaking of bread" than the Holy Supper instituted by Jesus Himself in the upper room on the night He was betrayed? No wonder these first Christians were so obstinate in their devotion to this fellowship. This was no support group or therapy session, after all. Theirs was a fellowship around the apostles' doctrine and the breaking of bread. It was fellowship around the Word and Sacrament, and

119

that meant it was actually fellowship with Jesus Himself. He had promised *Where two or three are gathered in My name, there am I in the midst of them* (Matt. 18:20 RSV).

I can see why the early church was so devoted to this holy Word and Sacrament; can you? Who wouldn't want to be where two or more are gathered in the name of Jesus, there to meet Him? If He is truly present in His Word and Sacrament as He claims to be, do you suppose we should persist obstinately in these things as well?

After all, as it was then, so it is now. Jesus Christ still stands in the midst of Christian congregations to teach them with His Holy Word. And He still sits at table to dine with lowly sinners in His Holy Supper. As it was in Jerusalem in the breaking of the bread, as it was in Jericho at the table of Zacchaeus, so it is each time we eat the bread and drink the cup of the Lord. Salvation comes to call. The bread of heaven comes down to feed us with His body once broken and to give us to drink of His blood once shed for the forgiveness of sins. And there is life in that blood; for it is the blood of God.

Devoted to the Prayers

I told you this chapter was about liturgical matters. But so far we've spent most of our time talking about the Word and the Sacraments. There's no other way to begin to talk about the liturgy, you see. For the only reason the church is devoted to the liturgy is because she is devoted to her Lord. Because she is devoted to her Lord, she is also devoted to His Holy Word and Sacrament. For in the Word and Sacrament the heavenly bridegroom comes to meet His earthly bride to feed and nourish her with His body given and His blood shed for her very life.

Not only was that first Christian congregation in Jerusalem devoted to the apostles' doctrine and breaking of bread; we also read that they were "devoted to the prayers," as St. Luke puts it in the plural. It's not just that these early Christians were accustomed to pray, but they were accustomed to pray in a certain way, with certain prescribed prayers; in other words, they had a liturgy.

This may come as a shock for some who think that early Christians gathered for worship generally in free-form settings, with each person praying as the spirit moved him. But we have to remember that Christianity didn't arrive in a vacuum. God built His New Testament church squarely on the foundation of the Old Testament.

Already at the very beginning of time *men began to call on the name of the LORD,* we read in Genesis (4:26). Throughout those early generations, at the time of Abraham and the other patriarchs, and then especially in the prescribed rituals for priestly sacrifice in the wilderness tabernacle and the temple on Mount Zion, God's people always had a liturgy. It was a liturgy of the Word of God.

The Breath of Life

By the word of the LORD were the heavens made, their starry host by the breath of his mouth, the Psalmist writes (33:6). *The LORD God formed the man from the dust of the ground and breathed into his nostrils the breath of life, and the man became a living being* (Gen. 2:7). All of life rests on the vivifying power of the Word of God and His Holy Spirit, the Giver of life.

As it was in the beginning, so it is now. As the Word of God was the source and the power of life in the first creation, so the Word of God is the source and power of life in the new creation by water and the Spirit. The eternal Word from the Father, through whom all things were made and without whom nothing was made that has been made, this very same Word was made flesh and dwelt among us, full of grace and truth, the only Son from the Father.

And that means we cannot discuss the liturgy apart from the incarnation of the Son of God in human flesh. The Incarnation is the sobering reminder that all talk about "invitational, entertaining, uplifting worship" must begin somewhere else. As we discuss "marketing the church" to the peculiar tastes of Americans at the end of the 20th century, we have to begin with this solemn 1st-century assumption: *You were dead in your transgressions and sins* (Eph. 2:1). We need more than just a lift; we need a resuscitation!

And so all liturgy begins at the beginning, with the astounding great good news that God has breathed His life into this world of death in the person of His Son, Jesus Christ, who is our life. He is the source and origin of all life. Not only in the creation of the cosmos, but also in the new creation of His holy bride, the church. As Eve was built from the flesh of Adam, so the Church originates in

121

the incarnate flesh of the Son of God. *In him was life, and that life was the light of men* (John 1:4). From the side of the second life-giving Adam poured forth blood and water in his death on the cross. But that very death is the source of life for the church in every age. *For there are three that testify: the Spirit, the water and the blood; and the three are in agreement. . . . And this is the testimony: God has given us eternal life, and this life is in his Son* (1 John 5:7–8, 11).

The incarnate Word of God is thus the focus of all worship and liturgy. He Himself is our life, and in the liturgy the Lord of life comes to our dying world to dispense His life hidden under the channels of washing, proclamation, and meal. The shepherds of Bethlehem have nothing over us. They went to the stable with hurried steps to gaze upon God lying in the hay. Yet each Lord's Day this same God born in Bethlehem, crucified, risen, and ascended to the Father's right hand lies hidden in the oral and tangible Word of His Gospel just as surely as He once lay in lowly infant disguise in the manger. And in the swaddling clothes of His Word and Sacrament our risen and ascended Lord continues to breathe life to all His people in every age.

The church has historically referred to God's Holy Word and Sacraments as the "means of grace." For these are the channels of Christ's redeeming love for us. Though we cannot go to Him, He comes to us through these instruments. Through these means He conveys to us the forgiveness, life, and salvation once earned for us on His cross. And in this dying world we cling to these channels for our very life; for without God's grace we would die in this wilderness.

Therefore in the liturgy the church serves as stewardess of the means of grace, serving up heaping portions of the forgiveness of sins, life, and salvation earned by her glorious Lord. The church has no life apart from the Word by which she was created. And the church has no life to impart to this dying world apart from that same life-giving Word of God.

The Church's Respiration

The liturgy is the church's breath. The fiber of the liturgy is the Gospel; its components are the very words of God. Therefore the liturgy breathes the life of the Gospel into the body of the church. In the liturgy the church inhales deeply of the life-giving breath of the Spirit. But in the liturgy the church also exhales; that is, she offers up to God her prayers.

Prayer is to faith as breath is to lungs. There can be no breath without lungs. But there can be lungs without breath—and they are dead lungs. True prayer cannot exist without faith, but faith that does not pray is dying. In other words, when the Giver of all life opens our mouth to receive the good gifts of His Holy Word, out of that same mouth flow petitions and praises. Thus the psalmist can write, *O Lord, open thou my lips, and my mouth shall show forth Thy praise* (51:15 KJV).

Healthy organisms not only inhale; they also exhale. So it is with church, the living organism created in Jesus Christ to be His holy bride and His living body in this world. In the liturgy the church inhales, and exhales as well. She both stands in the presence of God to receive His good gifts and also responds to Him in prayer and praise.

The church has no life apart from Christ. Her motto is the same as Paul's: *For to me, to live is Christ* (Phil. 1:21). The liturgy is the church's life first of all because there the living Lord comes to meet His holy bride. The liturgy is the church's life also because in the liturgy the bride gives herself to her heavenly Husband. The liturgy is filled with the life of Jesus Christ in His Word and Sacrament. Therefore the liturgy is both the foundation and the pattern of the Christian life. It is not only the source of the church's life in Christ, but also the shape of the church's life in Christ. It is the place where she draws her breath and where she gives it back again. It is where she inhales the life-giving power of the Spirit and where she exhales in the power of the Spirit.

In Spirit and in Truth

The woman at the well in Samaria wanted to debate with Jesus on questions of liturgical style; whether Mount Gerizim or Mount Zion was the proper place for worship. Jesus cut to the heart of the matter: *the hour is coming, and now is, when the true worshipers will worship the Father in spirit and truth, for such the Father seeks to worship Him* (John 4:23 RSV). It was a remarkable reply, loaded with liturgical implications for you and me. Though we like to be in control of our relationship with God, Jesus teaches us that genuine worship is always initiated by the Father, who actively seeks out worshipers. He also spells out the Trinitarian shape of the liturgy: genuine worship of the Father is done "in" the Spirit and the Son (who is the Way, and the Truth and the Life). True worshipers always worship the Father in Spirit and in Truth.

And so the Father continues to seek worshipers still in our day. As it was in Samaria, so it is now and ever will be in Christ's holy church. In His Word and Sacrament she first draws her breath and then gives it back again in her prayers. In this liturgical setting the church receives forgiveness of sins, life, and salvation *from* the Father *through* the Son *in* the power of the Spirit, and there she also offers her sacrifice of worship *in* the Spirit *through* the Son back *to* the Father.

The Assembly of the Lord

I mentioned that the liturgy is a liturgy of the Word of God. Let me explain. While it's true that the time-honored components of the historic liturgy are essentially distilled Scripture, I mean to say something more than that. To say that the liturgy is a liturgy of the Word of God is to say that the church is herself a creation of God, called into being by the power of God's creating Word. Likewise, she is summoned to praise by that very same Word of God.

Among us it is just as it was with Israel at Sinai. There God convened His people in solemn assembly by personal invitation through Moses:

> And Moses went up to God, and the LORD called to him out of the mountain, saying, "Thus you shall say to the house of Jacob, and tell the people of Israel: 'You have seen what I did to the Egyptians, and how I bore you on eagles' wings and brought you to Myself. Now therefore, if you will obey My voice and keep My covenant, you shall be My own possession among all peoples; for all the earth is Mine, and you shall be to Me a kingdom of priests and a holy nation.' These are the words which you shall speak to the children of Israel." (Ex. 19:3–6 RSV)

We should note that this convocation was called by God for the purpose of hearing God; the Lord gathered them together by His Word so that they could hear His Word. There on Sinai, amid fire and smoke and earthquake, the Lord Himself summoned His people to solemn assembly and spoke with His servant Moses. This assembly was brought about by God's Word in order to hear God's Word.

But the Sinai gathering was a long time ago and far away. What does that have to do with us Christians? More specifically, what does this gathering have to do with the Christian liturgy?

Life Together

The church is the New Testament people of God. And what God did for His Old Testament people, He continues to do for us. He summons His church by His Word in order to hear His Word. Yet there is no fear among us, as there was at Sinai. For the consuming fire of God's holy presence has already engulfed our sin at Calvary, where He made His Son to be sin for us. The Cross removes the terror of Sinai. We come calmly to the Father in peace and joy, for we approach Him through the Son in the power of the Spirit. We come together in the liturgy—as always—by His invitation, to hear His Word.

And there is no fear in the Word of His grace, for by that Word we live. We live as children of our heavenly Father, summoned from the death of sin to life in Christ. He calls us from our solitary prisons to live together in the liturgy in holy assembly as sons and daughters of the King, brothers and sisters all.

The liturgy rescues us from the tyranny of individualism, a particularly American heresy. You and I were never created to live alone, and yet so often the Gospel is presented as a way to become healthy, wealthy, or wise; a path toward self-improvement. We are told how to become better solo practitioners of the faith in our daily life, but we are not taught how to live together in the family of faith as redeemed sinners. Ironically, while we long for community, so much of Christian preaching and teaching drives wedges between us, focused as it often is so narrowly on the individual Christian life.

125

PART 3: THE LITURGICAL SHAPE

Biblical community transcends time and space; we are encouraged to leave behind our sight and rely on faith: *Set your minds on things above, not on earthly things* (Col. 3:2). In the worshiping congregation we are not alone; the saints who have gone ahead into heaven are still alive and with us in the fellowship of the church. Uniquely and especially in the liturgy we are surrounded by the company of this great cloud of witnesses. Misery loves company, and so does faith. In the divine service the worshiping congregation is part of a vast invisible company of believers, living and departed, who join in continual praise to the God of heaven and earth. This is the timeless community of faith.

In contrast, Christians are too often urged to seek their fellowship and encouragement in the contemporary community of experience. We are told to find our strength in the words and feelings of others who are like us; support groups masquerade as "Bible studies" in which the techniques of psychology and sociology steal the spotlight away from the Word of God.

True, Christian love and support are crucial to the faith: *Carry each other's burdens, and in this way you will fulfill the law of Christ* (Gal. 6:2). Still, we need community that is more than skin deep. The church is not a loose confederation of separate fellowship groups organized for special-interest groups, though that's probably what we'd prefer. For left to ourselves, most of us search out community with people who are just like us. But God loves us too much to abandon us to our inclinations; He provides us with a deeper fellowship. In the church He supplies us with a family of faith that transcends time and space. And week after week in the worshiping congregation He brings us all together for a reunion.

The liturgy removes the walls we erect around ourselves and the wedges others seek to drive between us and our brothers and sisters. In the liturgy God once again summons His people to solemn assembly. And when we come together, we discover we are not alone. For the one who calls us into fellowship with Him also calls us into fellowship with others, newly created as we are by the washing of water with the Word to be His sons and daughters.

The holy smoke of God's presence struck terror in the hearts of sinners at Sinai. But the Cross has intervened. And so for Christians there's no terror in the liturgy in the presence of God, for we are invited as His sons and daughters through faith in Christ. Still in the liturgy there are echoes of Sinai. For now, just as then, God creates a community by His Word in order to hear His Word. It is a holy convocation; an audience with the living God. And so we must realize the public liturgy is like no other public gathering.

In ordinary gatherings, leaders usually begin by developing rapport with the group before proceeding with the business at hand. But the liturgical assembly is no ordinary gathering. The pastor who leads us in worship needs no introduction. We know he is a child of God, one of us. But in this gathering he has a unique role. For we have called him to be a spokesman for God, to perform the sacred duties of God's holy ministry among us. Therefore we have little interest in personal rapport with him.

By ancient custom the church deliberately vests her pastors in clothing which hides their personal identity. Yet at the same time liturgical vestments identify pastors as authorized servants of God among His people. A pastor might appear and sound impersonal in the liturgy, but there's nothing more personal than what he does there. For pastors are spokesmen for God; stewards of God's holy mysteries proclaimed and dispensed among His people.

And so by the very call and invitation of God Himself, the pastor begins the liturgy by invoking that blessed name: *In the name of the Father and of the Son and of the Holy Spirit.* And by that name we live. For where God puts His name, He is there to bless with His presence. That holy name was first put upon us in our Baptism, where we were born again into the family of faith. And repeatedly, whenever and wherever we invoke the name of the Holy Trinity, He comes again to bless us with His presence.

And so over and over again in the liturgy it is the same: God summons His people to solemn assembly in His name. Though we live always in His presence, in the liturgy He is uniquely present with us. His Word and Sacrament throb with His presence. By His name He summons us, and we enter into His presence with joy: *Let us come into His presence with thanksgiving; let us make a joyful noise to Him with songs of praise* (Ps. 95:2 RSV).

Taking Off Our Shoes

The liturgical assembly is in the world, yet not of the world. Here heaven intersects with earth. And so, like Moses before us, we remove our shoes in the presence of God. We may speak and act a bit differently in the liturgy than we do ordinarily, but then we are in extraordinary circumstances. For the ground upon which we stand is holy ground. Whenever and wherever we step into the liturgy, we step on holy ground; we step into the presence of God.

The liturgy strikes some people as cold and impersonal, but that's because it is an extraordinary situation. Ritual for its own sake is idolatry, but even secular society has certain revered rituals. The formal changing of the guard at the Tomb of the Unknowns in Arlington Cemetery, for example, reinforces the solemn honor a grateful nation accords its dead heroes. No one calls the soldiers of the honor guard hypocrites because they act differently at those tombs than they would, say, at the beach or the movies. Solemn assembly calls for solemn actions.

But the solemn actions of the liturgy are not cold and impersonal. For we are never more at home than when we are with God. And we are never more ourselves than when we are in community with the brothers and sisters He has given us in the family of faith. Some of those siblings we know, but others are known only to God. Yet we are all blood relatives. By the precious blood of Christ we were rescued from our sins and made members of one family.

The Beauty of Holiness

Holy ground calls for holy songs. Yet some are put off by the foreign feel of the liturgy. Our ears are so jaded by the discord of modern life that the harmonious texts of the ancient liturgy seem stilted. Our voices are so attuned to the music of this age that the liturgy's timeless music seems awkward. Yet the genius of the historic liturgy is that it has always managed to transcend time and space. Changing ever so slowly through the centuries, it has borrowed something from every culture it has touched, and yet it has never been bound to any one of them.

Like a giant coral reef, the liturgy grows almost imperceptibly from the great deep with the accretions of the centuries. Unlike a coral reef, it teems with life throughout, the contributions of each succeeding age as alive as the one before it. The liturgy pulses with life. For there God speaks His Word. And there is life in that Word.

No wonder the liturgy seems foreign to us, then. For you and I live in a dying world, and the liturgy invites us to enter the land of the living. Like Isaiah before us, the prospect seems threatening. In the temple liturgy He was confronted with the presence of God. *Woe is me!* He exclaimed. *For I am lost; for I am a man of unclean lips, and I dwell in the midst of a people of unclean lips; for my eyes have seen the King, the LORD of hosts* (Is. 6:5 RSV). But with a burning coal from God's holy altar Isaiah's sin was purged: *Behold, this has touched your lips; your guilt is taken away, and your sin forgiven* (6:7 RSV).

As it was then, so it is now. In God's Holy Word and Sacrament the holiness of God eradicates our sin. Our guilt is taken away and our sin forgiven. That forgiveness always means the death of sin, and for that reason it is a fearful prospect. But by that death we live. And in the sacred liturgy we live most completely as God's holy people, singing the songs of Zion in this foreign land.

The foreignness of the liturgy is really a matter of perspective, you see. French-speaking people may feel out of place in Omaha, but they are at home in Paris. So too the language and the music of the liturgy may seem awkward to us, but that's because we spend so much time on alien turf we've learned to be at home in a foreign land. But the liturgy is where God's people belong. It is an outpost of the kingdom of God on the frontier of this world. *For here we do not have an enduring city, but we are looking for the city that is to come* (Heb. 13:14).

And so in the liturgy God's people learn once more to speak their native tongue, singing the songs of heaven on earth through Gospel-seared lips. There is a certain beauty to these songs, though it is a beauty not of this world: *Ascribe to the LORD the glory due his name; worship the LORD in the splendor of his holiness* (Ps. 29:2).

The Festal Gathering

Each Lord's Day in the holy liturgy history repeats itself. Once more God summons His people to holy convocation by His Holy

Word. Once more He opens up their lips, and from their mouth flows forth His praise. Thus His Holy Word is at one and the same time the vehicle of His saving grace and the vehicle of their praise as well.

At Sinai the mountain was shrouded in the holy smoke of the presence of God, and the air was pierced with thunder and lightening and the trumpet blast of His voice. Yet it was only a temporary convocation, a transient audience with God. In the liturgy you and I are invited into a permanent assembly that transcends heaven and earth. It is not the assembly of Sinai, but of Mount Zion—the holy city, the new Jerusalem. It is not an assembly of sinners filled with fear, but the joyful assembly of all the redeemed in heaven and earth.

In the sacred liturgy only the eyes and ears of faith can see God's presence and hear His voice. And yet He has placed His name on His Holy Word and Sacrament. And where His name is, there He is present to bless us with light and life in His incarnate Son. In the liturgy there is peace in this world, yet not of the world. We look not backward to Sinai, but forward to Zion. Therefore in the liturgy there is peace bought with blood—the peace of the Lord Jesus Christ, which transcends all human understanding. It is the peace of heaven itself, come down to earth:

> For you have not come to what may be touched, a blazing fire, and darkness, and gloom, and a tempest, and the sound of a trumpet, and a voice whose words made the hearers entreat that no further messages be spoken to them. . . . But you have come to Mount Zion and to the city of the living God, the heavenly Jerusalem, and to innumerable angels in festal gathering, and to the assembly of the first-born who are enrolled in heaven, and to a judge who is God of all, and to the spirits of just men made perfect, and to Jesus, the mediator of a new covenant, and to the sprinkled blood that speaks more graciously than the blood of Abel. (Heb. 12:18–19, 22–24 RSV)

There's no place like home. But the liturgy is not the land of Oz; it's our true home—the place where we belong. God's children are never more completely at home than when they hear His Word, receive His Sacrament, and sing His praise. Though restless in this world, in Him they have their final rest. And so in the liturgy there is rest in His presence along the way.

A Sabbath in the Wilderness

We all could use some rest along the way, that's for sure. Our pilgrimage gets tiresome. That's the way it was for Israel, too. Just two months out on their exodus from Egypt, they were already tired of their journey. They complained that Moses and Aaron had led them out of Egypt. They thought that death on a full stomach in slavery would be preferable to death on an empty stomach in freedom.

Remember how God fed them? He provided food for the journey; He gave them manna from heaven. But He also provided rest along the way. For along with the bread from heaven God also gave His people the Sabbath. It was a day of rest, not merely for weary bones, but for weary souls as well. All work ceased, to be sure. But more than that, it was a day of solemn rest, holy with the presence of God. On this day all the burdens of life could be laid down in sacred communion with the Creator; it was His loving gift to His people: *The Lord has given you the Sabbath* (Ex. 16:29).

We sell hamburgers and athletic shoes to frazzled consumers with a conscious appeal to self-appeasement: "You deserve a break today"; "Just do it." And these ads strike a chord with a lot of us in our harried world. Faster and faster we go, and yet we seem to be getting nowhere. We're prisoners of our technology; every labor-saving device we invent seems to add to our workload. Stress has become the hallmark of success, as we strive to do more and more in less and less time.

But far worse than the pressure of time is the burden of our hearts. Underneath our determined smiles there is heartache. For like Israel, we too are tired—and sick. We are tired of the mad pace at which we live and sick of the emptiness inside. We are sick all right, and our sickness is a sickness unto death.

Is there any rest in this wilderness? Yes there is—already; but not yet.

Rest Along the Way

There is a rest to come, that's for sure. One day we shall see God face to face. One day He shall wipe away all our tears with His own hand. One day we shall rest from all our labors in the eternal heavenly Sabbath. There in heaven's glory our restlessness shall cease, for we shall find our final rest in God. There the evening of all our Sabbaths shall dawn into an eternal Easter Day, when we shall know as we are known. There we shall be full of Him who is already our fullness in every way.

Then we'll know experientially what we already personally believe: *Be still, and know that I am God* (Ps. 46:10). But not yet. Right now every believer walks by faith, not by sight. We get anxious and troubled about many things. We lay our burdens down, only to pick them up again.

Yet already there is a Sabbath rest for all God's own. It is the rest He provides in the sacred liturgy, where by His invitation we enter His eternal, heavenly rest already here in this harried world.

> So then, there remains a Sabbath rest for the people of God; for whoever enters God's rest also ceases from his labors as God did from his. (Heb. 4:8–10 RSV)

Our Sabbath Rest

Come to me, invites Jesus, *all you who are weary and burdened.* And we're all ears. For that's us: weary and burdened. He has a solution for our weary burdens, and it has nothing to do with gaining control or taking a break from the hassles of life. For the holy rest of God is to be found in Jesus Christ Himself:

> I will give you rest. Take my yoke upon you, and learn from me; for I am gentle and humble in heart, and you will find rest for your souls. (Matt. 11:28–29)

Here's the secret to survival in the wilderness of this world: the church in every age has found rest in her glorious Lord. In Jesus Christ all liturgical regulations of the Old Testament—including the Sabbath Day itself—find their fulfillment. Jesus Christ is the true Sabbath of God.

> Therefore do not let anyone judge you by what you eat or drink, or with regard to a religious festival, a New Moon celebration or a Sabbath day. These are a shadow of the things that were to come; the reality, however, is found in Christ. (Col. 2:16–17)

In Christ we have rest in all our wildernesses. *Peace be with you,* He said to His disciples, fresh from His grave on Easter evening. *When He had said this, He showed them His hands and His side* (John 20:19, 20 RSV).

"Peace be with you" is the repeated refrain of the ancient liturgy. And this is no pious wish, but reality. For the Lord who showed the wounds in His living body gives us that same body and His precious blood in His Holy Supper. Thus we find rest and refreshment in the sacred liturgy; there we are at peace in Him who is our peace.

And that peace surpasses all human understanding.

A Song to Sing

Ancient Israel had many ups and downs, but in Babylon Israel was really in the pits. Exiled from their homeland, the Israelites lived as strangers in a strange land. That was bad enough. But worst of all they were alienated from the temple of the Lord on Mount Zion in Jerusalem. With broken hearts, they sat and wept the tears only a refugee can know:

> By the rivers of Babylon we sat and wept when we remembered Zion. There on the poplars we hung our harps, for there our captors asked us for songs, our tormentors demanded songs of joy; they said, "Sing us one of the songs of Zion!" How can we sing the songs of the LORD while in a foreign land? (Ps. 137:1–4)

We know their pain; for every child of God is a refugee in this world. Here in the shadow of death the church lives in exile, longing for the life only God can give. Our songs of joy are sometimes sung with broken hearts, heavy with the heartache of sin. Israel's poignant question is ours as well: *How can we sing the songs of the LORD while in a foreign land?*

In this foreign land we're prisoners of our emotions. Sometimes we're up, sometimes we're down. No wonder our praises and prayers can be erratic at times; it's hard to sing the songs of Zion when you live in a foreign land.

But here on the foreign turf of this world Christ's church has a song to sing. The sacred liturgy rescues us from the tyranny of our emotions; in the liturgy God Himself teaches us what to pray. His

Word summons us to praise and His Word is also the vehicle of our praise. And there is joy once more.

In the liturgy God Himself gives His church a song to sing in this fallen world. It is a song of holy solemnity, for it is a song full of the presence of God:

> You shall have a song as in the night when a holy feast is kept; and gladness of heart, as when one sets out to the sound of the flute to go to the mountain of the LORD, to the Rock of Israel. And the Lord will cause His majestic voice to be heard. . . . (Is. 30:29–30 RSV)

Every time we gather for the divine service history repeats itself. Once again the majestic voice of the Lord is heard, announcing the grace and truth that are in Jesus Christ. Once again God's Word summons His people in holy assembly to hear God's Word. And this vehicle of His Word is also the vehicle of our praise. We speak as we are spoken to; God speaks to us in grace and blessing, and we respond in prayer and praise. The cycle is forever the same. The grace and blessing are the Father's; given freely through the Son in the power of the Holy Spirit. Thus our prayers and praises are also His; returned in the Spirit through the Son to the Father.

God with Us

And so the essence of our liturgical life together is the real presence of the living Lord of the church with His earthly bride. He gives us a song to sing here in this foreign land. He who once took up residence in human flesh now gives His heavenly power hidden in the lowly human word of His holy Gospel—and, wonder of wonders, once again God dwells among His people in that holy Word. Thus the best liturgical direction the apostle can give the Colossian church is to remind them what's actually going on in their prayers and praises:

> Let the word of Christ dwell in you richly as you teach and admonish one another with all wisdom, and as you sing psalms, hymns and spiritual songs with gratitude in your hearts to God. (Col. 3:16)

In His Word both spoken and sung, Christ dwells in the midst of the worshiping congregation. When Christ is present, His people acknowledge His presence with appropriate behavior. We stand, we sit, we kneel, we bow. It's not the way we normally act, but holy ground calls for holy action. And the liturgy of public worship is certainly holy ground; for the living Lord is present with His assembled church in His Holy Word and Sacrament.

And where the Lord is present, there is peace for all His own.

The Distant Triumph Song

The church's terrestrial song is an echo here of the celestial hymn. She lives on earth, but she sings of heaven. In a world intent on the here and now, she points to the then and there. In a world consumed with things below, she longs for things above.

> For, as I have often told you before and now say again even with tears, many live as enemies of the cross of Christ. Their destiny is destruction, their god is their stomach, and their glory is in their shame. Their mind is on earthly things. But our citizenship is in heaven. And we eagerly await a Savior from there, the Lord Jesus Christ, who, by the power that enables him to bring everything under his control, will transform our lowly bodies so that they will be like his glorious body. (Phil. 3:18–21)

Yet the church is not so heavenly minded she is of no earthly good. For her mission in this world is the mission of the Father in heaven. *As the Father has sent me, I am sending you,* said Jesus to His disciples (John 20:21). And so it has always been in Christ's church. Rescue leads to praise, and praise to rescue. Liturgy always empowers mission, and mission always leads back to liturgy.

There's no separating the liturgical life of the church from the mission of the church; they are organically one piece. The two find common nourishment in the incarnate flesh of Jesus Christ, who is our life. As the Father sent Him, so He sends His church, cleansing her by water and the Spirit to be His holy bride. And so, for as long as she is in this dying world, the church proclaims her heavenly Husband's life-giving invitation:

> The Spirit and the bride say, "Come!" And let him who hears say, "Come!" Whoever is thirsty, let him come; and whoever wishes, let him take the free gift of the water of life. (Rev. 22:17)

Here on earth the church's song is part of Christ's heavenly mission. She proclaims the life that comes from the Father through the Son in the power of the Spirit, and she sings her praise in the Spirit through the Son back to the Father. And so in earthly tongues she sings the songs of heaven. The church sings continually here on earth the distant, triumphant song of those whose rest is won. And hearts are brave again, and arms are strong; for in that song the Lord causes His majestic voice to be heard. And there is gladness of heart once more.

For the church's song is her testimony in this dying world to her living Lord and the Life that is in Him alone. The church's song is as old as creation, when *the morning stars sang together and all the angels shouted for joy* (Job 38:7). It is the song of Moses at the Red Sea: *"I will sing to the LORD, for he is highly exalted. The horse and its rider he has hurled into the sea"* (Ex. 15:1).

And yet that song, no matter how old, is forever new. The church's song is a foretaste here of the eternal wedding banquet, where death and night are no more, and forever and forever the angels and archangels and all the company of heaven join ceaselessly to sing the song of the Lamb: *"Worthy is the Lamb who was slain, to receive power and wealth and wisdom and might and honor and glory and blessing"* (Rev. 5:12 RSV).

There is life in that song; for there is life in the Lamb.

8

Private Prayer: Liturgical Life Alone

Pray without ceasing. (1 Thess. 5:17 KJV)

The stockholders were nervous. The executive office door stood closed; its heavy wood and shining brass seemed to symbolize the impenetrable authority that sat ensconced inside. The chief had a powerful reputation, but some considered him quite remote. Would their petitions even be heard, much less granted? They turned to the manager, fearful yet hopeful.

"When you pray," replied Jesus, say "Our Father who art in heaven . . ."

The Presence of God

There is nothing more vital for the child of God than to be in His presence. Separate a toddler from its parent, and you have a frightened child. No wonder we live such fretful lives, then. For so often we attempt to go on alone, apart from our Father in heaven. Yet *in him we live and move and have our being* (Acts 17:28). No wonder our hearts are restless in this dying world; they long for rest in the one who is our life. We are restless until we find our rest in Him.

God's heart yearns for all His restless children. And so He works ceaselessly to prepare His people to stand in His presence:

Who may ascend the hill of the LORD? Who may stand in his holy place? He who has clean hands and a pure heart, who does not lift up his soul to an idol or swear by what is false. (Ps. 24:3–4)

Of all the men who've ever lived, only one qualifies by those standards to stand in the presence of God: Our Lord Jesus Christ. He was—and is—one of us; with flesh and bones like ours. Yet as

God's sinless Son, His hands are clean, and His heart is pure. Of all the sons and daughters of Adam, He alone rightfully belongs in the presence of God.

Yet, baptized into His body, by faith you and I also are God's adopted children. Heaven is our home, too. Cleansed in Christ's redeeming blood, our hands are just as clean as His, and our hearts as pure. And now we may stand in God's holy place, forgiven, whole, and free. That's where we belong: in the presence of God. Not just one day in heaven's glory, but also here and now in this dying world we have life in the presence of God.

The real presence of God, you see, is the heart and center of Christian living. You and I are not left here in this world to struggle on as best we can, rising above the sorrow and the heartaches of life by our own sheer determination. For we are not abandoned orphans, left here on the doorstep of this sinful world to live the holy life as best we can. We are sons of God. Male and female alike, we are all adopted as sons in Christ Jesus. Baptized into Christ, we have put on Christ.

> For in Christ Jesus you are all sons of God, through faith. For as many of you as were baptized into Christ have put on Christ. There is neither Jew nor Greek, there is neither slave nor free, there is neither male nor female; for you are all one in Christ Jesus. (Gal. 3:26–28 RSV)

At one time or another in childhood most of us played "dress-up." But our Baptism is no child's play. In that washing of water with the Word, you and I were actually clothed with Christ. We're not just masquerading; His righteousness is our proper apparel. Clothed in God's Son, we have all the rights of sonship, which includes intimate access to God. And that access is always the same: to the Father through the Son in the Spirit.

As it is in the public liturgy of the worshiping congregation, so it is in the private liturgy of our personal prayer and devotion. The Lord first opens our mouth, then from that same mouth pours forth our praise. The Trinitarian shape of the liturgy governs all our prayers and praises. The Father continually seeks worshipers through the Son in the Spirit, and we worship the Father in the Spirit through the Son.

The Liturgical Heart

Home is where we belong. And you and I as sons of God belong in the presence of God. That's what the Gospel of Jesus Christ is all about: the presence of God. The Nicene Creed lays out three wonderful realities that belong to every member of Christ's holy church: the forgiveness of sins, the resurrection of the body, and the life everlasting. This is the glorious future of all the children of God. It's all contained already here and now in the forgiveness of sins, but its culmination will be in eternity, where we will join in the ceaseless heavenly liturgy:

> Worthy is the Lamb who was slain, to receive power and wealth and wisdom and might and honor and glory and blessing! (Rev. 5:12 RSV)

No wonder, then, that the Athanasian Creed defines the universal Christian faith liturgically: "the catholic faith is this, that we *worship* [italics added] one God in three persons and three persons in one God." The Holy Trinity is Himself the very heart of the faith; the Father who first created the church has redeemed her by the blood of His Son and then sanctified her by His Spirit to be His holy dwelling. All we are and all we have received comes from the Father, through the Son, in the Holy Spirit. And all we do flows from who we are and what we have received. And so the entire Christian life—public worship, private prayer, and daily vocation—flows back in the Spirit through the Son to the Father, one God, now and forever. We live each day and to all eternity in the very presence of God. This is liturgical living; it's the only way to live.

But we aren't always aware of that, are we? We get so caught up in the "real" world that we forget who we actually are as children of God. Our heads do not naturally bow in humility; our knees do not naturally bend in worship; our hands do not naturally join in prayer. Our lives are so filled with other things that there is no room to be filled with God. And so like rats in a maze, we keep on wandering, but never arriving. We may not realize it, but we're on a fitful search for tranquility.

But God does not abandon us to frenzy. He gives us solace and peace and holy rest in His presence. That's why we go to church. In the sacred liturgy we are invited into the presence of God, who is present always with us. Yet as we all know, the Christian life is not lived exclusively within the four walls of a church building. We cannot always be in church. Therefore God's people have always prized personal prayer, for it is a private liturgy where we find rest and solace in the presence of God.

Getting Out of Ourselves

Left to ourselves here in this world, we become bogged down in mundane routine and paralyzed by our own fears. Prayer is the invitation to leave fear and routine behind and to enter again and again into our true identity as the children of God—to "ask Him as dear children ask their dear Father," as Luther put it. No apprehensions here, no holding back. Throwing caution to the wind, we rush in where angels fear to tread: to the very throne of God, there to offer the prayers and praises of our broken hearts in the confidence of His healing love. Our focus is not on our fears, but on our gracious God. We need not tremble before Him, for there is peace in Christ. Because of His love, our prayers are always the same—to the Father, through the Son, in the Spirit:

> [Christ] came and preached peace to you who were far off and peace to those who were near; for through Him we both have access in one Spirit to the Father. (Eph. 2:17–18 RSV)

In the Name of Jesus

It would be foolhardy for sinners to advance into the presence of God apart from the intervention of His Son, who is our peace. He has removed the wrath of the Father by being made a curse for us. He has ended the war between the Creator and His rebellious creation; the peace treaty is signed in His own blood. By His innocent suffering and death and with His holy, precious blood, He has earned the rights of sonship for every penitent sinner.

> If anybody does sin, we have one who speaks to the Father in our defense—Jesus Christ, the Righteous One. He is the atoning sacrifice for our sins, and not only for ours but also for the sins of the whole world. (1 John 2:1–2)

It is because of the Son of God that the children of God may address Him as Father. Apart from the intervention of Jesus Christ, we would know Him only as our judge.

Like Father, like Son—so the saying goes. But in the case of Jesus, it's the other way around. As the Son is in this world, so is the Father in heaven. *Anyone who has seen me has seen the Father,* Jesus informed His friends (John 14:9). Little children often confuse God the Son with God the Father. And we can understand why. For Jesus is the one who reveals the Father to us. The only God we know in this world is the one who was made flesh for us. The only God we love is the one who first loved us, laying down His life for us upon the cross.

In the first two parts of this book we've investigated the incarnational foundation of the Christian life and its sacramental focus; what God first accomplished in the flesh of His only-begotten Son He extends to us in, with, and under the washing, word, and meal He has given to His church on earth. This Christ-centered foundation and focus breathes life into the liturgical shape of the Christian life as well. Redeemed and recreated in the Son to be sons of God, we come boldly into the presence of God. Cleansed in His holy baptismal bath, we offer up the sacrifices of our prayers, our praises, and our lives in His service.

> Therefore, brothers, since we have confidence to enter the Most Holy Place by the blood of Jesus, by a new and living way opened for us through the curtain, that is, his body, and since we have a great priest over the house of God, let us draw near to God with a sincere heart in full assurance of faith, having our hearts sprinkled to cleanse us from a guilty conscience and having our bodies washed with pure water. (Heb. 10:19–22)

No need to worry that God might not accept what we bring Him. Our prayers, praises, and our very bodies are living sacrifices to God, holy and acceptable to Him through faith in Jesus Christ. That's why all our prayers (both public and private) and everything we do in our daily life as well—our entire liturgical life—is offered to the Father through the Son.

> Let the word of Christ dwell in you richly as you teach and admonish one another with all wisdom, and as you sing psalms, hymns and spiritual songs with gratitude in your hearts to God.

And whatever you do, whether in word or deed, do it all in the name of the Lord Jesus, giving thanks to God the Father through him. (Col. 3:16–17)

"In the name of Jesus." If you've grown up in the church, you've heard this liturgical formula all your life. But it is no mere formula; it is the lifeblood of all the children of God. All we do in this world as His children: our good works, our public worship and our private prayers—it's all one grand liturgical offering acceptable to God through the cleansing blood of His Son.

If we want to learn to pray we must become like children. For that's who we really are, children of God by faith in Christ Jesus. Thus the first step in prayer is to step into the presence of God our loving Father as His beloved children. And there's only one way to do that: in the name of Jesus.

What a Friend

Here is confidence for doubting hearts; here is comfort in all our fears. For Jesus Christ puts skin and bones on the love of God the Father. *God is Spirit,* Jesus taught the Samaritan woman, *and his worshipers must worship in spirit and in truth* (John 4:24). It may be hard for physical people to worship a Spirit; but when we come to the Father through the Son, we have a tangible channel for our prayers and praises.

Risen and ascended to the Father's right hand, He continually intercedes for all His own. We have a friend in high places! And Jesus still bears our human flesh and blood in heaven's high court. Therefore He knows our life inside and out.

There is comfort in human friendship, having someone who knows our heart, who feels our hurt and shares our pain. When such a friend says: "I understand," there is comfort in that compassion. But when that friend goes on to say: "I'm praying for you," there is genuine healing. It is the healing of God.

Jesus, our friend at the heavenly throne, is one who knows our heart intimately well. He knows our pain firsthand. He has walked the planet earth in skin and bones and knows the full range of human emotion. And not just the happier emotions; He is a man of sorrows and well acquainted with grief. He did not leave His humanity behind when He ascended to the Father's throne. True man as well as true God, while He intercedes for us He knows our heart and feels our pain.

> For we do not have a high priest who is unable to sympathize with our weaknesses, but we have one who has been tempted in every way, just as we are—yet was without sin. Let us then approach the throne of grace with confidence, so that we may receive mercy and find grace to help us in our time of need. (Heb. 4:15–16)

And so we come boldly to God as His children. We call upon His name in every trouble. We pray, praise, and give thanks to the Father in the Spirit through the Son; we pray in Jesus' name.

Learning to Pray

Prayer does not come naturally to the human heart. Since it is the language of faith, it must be learned just as we learn to speak— by imitation. We all learned to talk by mimicking the sounds of an adult. First the basics: "mama" and "dada"—then came the rest of our vocabulary. But it all begins with those first syllables, the most important sounds in our language. Adult speech can be likened to a giant skyscraper, the whole structure resting on the unseen foundations of infant speech. The entire edifice of our adult vocabulary is built on those earliest sounds by which we invoked the presence of the most important people in our infant world: "mama" or "dada."

It should come as no surprise to us that people don't know how to pray. The disciples of Jesus didn't know either. They had to ask: *"Lord, teach us to pray."* True prayer must be learned. And it is learned the same way we learn all other speech; by imitation. Thus when Jesus set out to teach His disciples to pray, He began with the basics. *"When you pray,"* He taught them, *"pray: 'Our Father in heaven' "* (Matt. 6:7, 9)

Linguists point out that the simplest vocables for *mother* and *father* in every culture are strikingly alike from one language to another. They're always words easily formed by infant lips. Little Hebrew children learned to call their fathers "abba," easily recognized as first cousin to our English word *dada*. This is how the baptized learn to pray. The Father invites us into His presence through the Son in the power of the Holy Spirit, and so we come to Him as beloved children, using the intimate language of infancy:

> Because you are sons, God sent the Spirit of his Son into our hearts, the Spirit who calls out, "Abba, Father." (Gal. 4:6)

So we are taught. And so we begin to pray: *Our Father in heaven*.

The Fellowship of Prayer

It's interesting that Jesus taught us to pray "our" Father, and not "my" Father. That's the way you and I would have started out if it were up to us: "*My* Father, give *me my* daily bread." We grab for what we want, not waiting for it to be passed. Impatiently we ask only for ourselves.

Jesus teaches us to pray otherwise. It's not just that He wants us to learn good manners; He wants to teach us that we belong to a family. Hence the plural pronouns in the prayer He taught, which is foundational to all Christian prayer. "The Our Father," some call it. Others call it "The Lord's Prayer." Both names are appropriate, for in this prayer the Lord of the church teaches all the baptized to pray together with one voice to their true Father in heaven.

Gathered with the faithful in church, it's easy to see the wisdom of this prayer. There we can see others who address God as Father; and so when we open our mouths together to pray, it comes naturally to say, "Our Father." Not so when we're alone. Then we're inclined to say: "Lord, I just want to tell you . . ."

But what is foundational to corporate prayer is also foundational to private prayer. You and I in our private devotions are as much involved in the family of faith as when we're gathered with others in the Christian congregation. Not that "I" and "me" are inappropriate in private prayers. But our personal prayer is always offered in unison with the people of God everywhere. Though we might be separated from the congregation, we never pray alone. All Christendom prays along with us, and there is strength in such company. The fellowship of other Christians provides encouragement to faith.

The first Christian congregation in Jerusalem was devoted to "the fellowship . . . and to the prayers." And we know why. There is strength in numbers. The sight of a Christian brother or sister is encouragement in itself, but only as an outward sign. Our true fellowship is unseen, the fellowship of hearts knit as one by the Spirit of God by faith in Jesus Christ. Our whole life in this world is a life in and through the Word of God.

The apostle prayed that the Ephesians Christians might have faith to behold a community invisible to the naked eye:

> I pray that you, being rooted and established in love, may have power, together with all the saints, to grasp how wide and long and high and deep is the love of Christ, and to know this love that surpasses knowledge—that you may be filled to the measure of all the fullness of God. (Eph. 3:17–19)

This is the height and depth the liturgy brings to our personal prayers: the length and width of the community of faith.

This communal dimension to personal prayer cannot be overemphasized in our time. Our culture encourages us to think of ourselves as independent entities. With all of our advanced technology in communications, we lead increasingly lonely lives. Some of our barriers we erect out of self-defense, others are the products of our environment.

But when we define personal prayer as liturgical prayer, we begin to knock down all barriers to genuine community, whether self-chosen or imposed. For when we learn to pray as Jesus taught, we learn that all prayer is corporate prayer, whether in church or by ourselves. We always pray in fellowship with the church even when we pray alone.

So the Lord Jesus teaches us. Thus when we open our mouths to pray, we speak as we were spoken to. We pray as we were taught. We pray individually as beloved children to a loving Father in company with our siblings in the faith: *Abba . . . ; Our Father in Heaven.*

By Word and by Prayer

If we don't instinctively know how to pray, we don't know what to pray, either. Both must be taught. Left to ourselves, we would pray all by ourselves, out of the shallow selfishness of our sinful hearts. It is God who teaches us to pray in the company of others.

PART 3: THE LITURGICAL SHAPE

But just as God teaches us to pray together even when we're alone, He also teaches us what to pray about. Here again our selfishness gets in the way. Left to ourselves, we would pray out of the fleeting emotions of the moment. God teaches us to pray from the depths of His Word.

Remember, we speak to God as we are spoken to. Not only does He teach us how to address Him, but He teaches us what to say. He puts His own Word in our mouth, and we pray it back to Him. That's why there is a liturgical shape also to private prayer; it rescues us from the tyranny of our emotions.

Think for a moment what communication would be like if every person had to invent a personal language. If we relied on our instincts alone, our speech would be limited to whatever sounds we could muster to convey what we felt at the time. We've already seen how we learn to speak by imitating the sounds of our parents. Adult language is constructed on the building blocks of vocables first shaped on our infant lips. As we grew older, we came to attach meaning to those early sounds, gradually adding new words until we have a whole warehouse of language with which we can describe reality.

Now consider the words you use in prayer. Do you find yourself continually praying "I" language? "Lord, I just want to tell you . . . ," "Lord, I'm feeling . . . ," "Lord, I need . . . ," or—perhaps most revealing of all: "Lord, I want . . ." Such language in prayer is not wrong. Like any parent, our Father in heaven delights to hear His children speak to Him, even in infant language. But like other parents, our heavenly Father desires to see our vocabulary grow. So He gives us His Word, by which He teaches us not only how to pray, but what to pray.

And when we learn to speak to God as He speaks to us, we quickly move beyond "I" language to "You" language. We begin prayer with God and the sure promises of His Word, not with ourselves and our flimsy emotions. Notice in the prayer Jesus teaches us to pray we speak to God about His name, His kingdom, and His will before we ever get around to praying about ourselves.

One of the most helpful hints for personal prayer I've ever heard is this one: after your opening address, let the first word out of your mouth be "You." Speak to God about who He is and what

He has done. Describe Him as He has revealed Himself in His Word. Give Him praise and honor; repeat back to Him what He has taught you in His Holy Word. You'll find, as I have, that "You" language in prayer lends confidence for the "I" language.

However you begin, remember that God's children always begin at the beginning, with God. We speak as we are spoken to. He opens up our mouths, and out comes the Word He gives us to speak. The vocabulary of prayer is formed by the Word of God Himself. There is strength in such prayer, for it is prayer grounded in the very name of God. And where God's name is, there He is to bless with His presence. All liturgical prayer, whether public or private, is grounded in the conviction that God is present in His Word.

> I will bow down toward your holy temple and will praise your name for your love and your faithfulness, for you have exalted above all things your name and your word. When I called, you answered me; you made me bold and stouthearted. (Ps. 138:2–3)

God's Prayer Book

When we open the book of Psalms, the Psalter, we quickly discover we are over our heads in prayer. From beginning to end, from the heights of exultation to the pits of despair, every psalm is a prayer. Their poetic structure and editorial notations indicate that most of them were designed to be sung. The very name *psalm* means "song," in fact. More about singing and prayer later.

For now, please note that in the Psalter God has provided us with a ready-made prayer book. Here again, such prayer does not come naturally. You and I aren't given to praying the words of others, even if it is the Word of God. We're much more comfortable saying what's on our heart than saying a psalm.

All great women and men of prayer, however, have learned to use the psalms as the root of prayer life. Just as the church has drawn on the wellsprings of the psalms for her public liturgy, so Christians through the ages have relied on the psalms as the heart of their personal prayers.

Many who use the psalms in private devotion treat them as a kind of spiritual catalog, thumbing through the Psalter until they find one that expresses their feelings of the moment. I was no exception; I used to hunt for a psalm that said what I felt. Indeed, there is comfort in that method of praying the psalms. I've come to see, however, that the psalms do not only reflect my experiences; they reveal the experience of Jesus Christ Himself. And so now I've quit paging through them. I use a prescribed lectionary that includes a suggested psalm or psalms appropriate to the liturgical year. This system of prayer gives access directly to heart of our Lord, who suffered all that we suffer—and far more. And it reveals His profound joy—which is beyond all that we could ever imagine.

The Cycle of Prayer

Just a word about the liturgical year. I promised you this book was not about liturgical form, and I'd like to keep my promise. However, the liturgical year is fundamental to what we're exploring in this chapter; yet it happens to be one of the best-kept secrets in Christendom, even among liturgical churches.

In my tradition we deck our altars and other church furnishings with colored cloths called paraments. Many parishioners watch the change of colors year after year—white at Christmas and Easter, Red at Pentecost, etc.—and yet have only a vague conception of what this liturgical cycle is all about.

Here again, there are plenty of good books available on the history and meaning of the church year. For now, suffice it to say that this annual cycle has come to be a crucial teaching tool for countless millions of Christians. It teaches us how Christian faith and life are intertwined. It teaches us about God the Holy Trinity and how time and eternity intersect in Him. It teaches us how the time of this world is permeated by the timeless work of God: Father, Son, and Holy Spirit.

From the Father, through the Son, in the Spirit, and then back again. This is the path of the church's prayer, and this is the route traced by the liturgical year. The liturgical year can be divided into three segments. First, the Time of Christmas, celebrating the gift of God the Father who sent His Son in the power of the Spirit to accomplish our salvation. Then the Time of Easter, featuring the work of the Son who by the power of the Spirit obeyed His Father all the way to death on the cross, completing our salvation by His resurrection from the dead on the third day. Finally, Pentecost, the Time of the Church, highlights the work of the Holy Spirit in dispensing all that the Father accomplished through the Son.

Notice how it all fits together? The threeness of the church year comes together into one. Triple activity, one reality. It's no accident, for that's the kind of God we have: Father, Son, and Spirit; one God, now and forever. Jesus describes how it is with the Holy Trinity: What the Father designed, the Son accomplished and the Holy Spirit delivers:

> All that belongs to the Father is mine. That is why I said the Spirit will take from what is mine and make it known to you. (John 16:15)

There you have it. From the Father, through the Son, in the Spirit: life in all its fullness. Life forever with God in the timelessness of heaven, but life also here in the time of this world. It's all the same life, and it all centers in Jesus Christ, who is our life.

Your Personal Road Map

I would recommend highly the liturgical year as an excellent road map for your Christian pilgrimage. Year by year it will lead you back to retrace the steps of our Lord in earning our salvation. And yet year by year this same route leads you onward toward the heavenly goal, growing in the grace and holiness of Christ.

What appears to be a circular route is in fact the straightest path for the Christian life. How else can we advance except by retreating regularly to the source of our strength? In its cycle of fasts and feasts, the liturgical year leads us always back to Christ, who is our life, and then forward again into His service.

Thus the liturgical life echoes the rhythm of the universe. There's an annual cycle to the seasons, to be sure. But within the greater cycle are also smaller cycles; a monthly ebb and flow reflected in the tides and weather that the civilized world tends to overlook. Insulating ourselves in air-conditioned environments and artificially dispelling the darkness of night, we avoid the regular cycles of the created order of things: seedtime and harvest, cold and heat, summer and winter, day and night.

The appointed psalms of the liturgical year lead us back home where we belong: into the presence of God as His dear children. We learn again what it is to pray within the shelter of His love as our Creator. We take another look around us and see that we fit within the broader circle of the rest of creation: mountain heights, valley depths, the sea and the dry land alike—all are props in the great drama of salvation God has unfolded. And we have a starring role:

> Come, let us sing for joy to the LORD; let us shout aloud to the Rock of our salvation. Let us come before him with thanksgiving and extol him with music and song. For the LORD is the great God, the great King above all gods. In his hand are the depths of the earth, and the mountain peaks belong to him. The sea is his, for he made it, and his hands formed the dry land. Come, let us bow down in worship, let us kneel before the LORD our Maker; for he is our God and we are the people of his pasture, the flock under his care. (Ps. 95:1–7)

Evening and Morning

When we begin to see that we are the flock under God's care, this world becomes a lot friendlier place to live in. When we begin to recognize that our frantic scurrying will not add one day to the length of our lives or make us one bit happier and fulfilled, we begin to relax. We find our rest in Him who is our peace. And His peace surpasses all human understanding.

Tying our prayers to the Word of God, we learn to relinquish control of our lives to the one who knows us best. After all, He created us to be His own, redeemed us with the blood of His Son, and sanctified us as His dwelling place. The Word He speaks to us in the Psalms we pray back to Him. Thus all of life is consecrated by the Word of God and by prayer. We discover that our Father in heaven designed our daily routine to be a cycle; we are the ones who've made it a rat race.

Exhausted by our daily work, we're invited each day to find rest for our bodies in sleep and rest for our souls within the shelter of Christ's peace: *I will lie down and sleep in peace, for you alone, O LORD, make me dwell in safety* (Ps. 4:8). Awaking, we find the creation up and running. We slip into the stream of life each day confident of God's continued presence: *In the morning, O LORD, you hear my voice; in the morning I lay my requests before you and wait in expectation.* (Ps. 5:3)

You and I tend to get things backward; we think of the day as beginning at dawn and ending in the evening, a mad race with the clock. The Word of God teaches us otherwise. *And there was evening, and there was morning—the first day* (Gen. 1:5).

Since ancient times Christians have always found the evening hours particularly conducive for prayer. As the evening lights were lit to dispel the darkness, they were reminded of Jesus Christ, who is the light of the world, the light no darkness can overcome. As they went to their rest, they were reminded of Jesus Christ, who invites all the faithful to find their rest in Him. As they laid down to sleep, they were reminded that sleep is rehearsal for the day of death, when they would lay down in this world only to rise again on the day of the resurrection of all flesh.

Still, whether we live or whether we die, we are the Lord's. An ancient evening prayer breathes the quiet confidence of all the faithful: "Guide us waking, O Lord, and guard us sleeping that awake we may watch with Christ and asleep we may rest in peace."

And so Christians begin the day: first quiet contemplation and confident prayer, then restful sleep. Refreshed in body and spirit, we rise to face the rest of the day. This is the rhythm of prayer that governs our life. It's when we allow our life to govern our prayer that you and I get into difficulty. For the chaos of life can wreak havoc with the rhythm of prayer.

And so the Christian life has a liturgical shape; not that prayer makes us Christians, but rather that Christians pray. Prayer is not a means of grace; it is not a channel for God's forgiving love to come to us. But prayer does have the command and promise of God; it is the way Christians go to their Father in heaven. He both directs and invites us to pray. And by this invitation our Father invites us into His presence, where our private prayers mingle with the public prayers and praises of the church in earth and heaven. And these prayers are all one; one perpetual liturgy continually offered up to the Father through the Son in the power of the Spirit, one God, now and forever.

Our private prayers might be liturgical life alone, but we are never alone at our prayers!

The Prayers of Jesus

Once you get involved in praying the Psalms, it isn't long before you begin to see that you're praying someone else's prayers. Each of the Psalms has a historical setting within the Old Testament era, some more obvious than others. It isn't hard to recognize David's anguished cry for forgiveness, for example, in the words of Psalm 51: *Hide your face from my sins and blot out all my iniquity. Create in me a pure heart, O God, and renew a steadfast spirit within me.*

Other Psalms, however, are more difficult to place within history. What are we to make of these strange words, for instance?

> I am poured out like water, and all my bones are out of joint. My heart has turned to wax; it has melted away within me. My strength is dried up like a potsherd, and my tongue sticks to the roof of my mouth; you lay me in the dust of death. Dogs have surrounded me; a band of evil men has encircled me, they have pierced my hands and my feet. I can count all my bones; people stare and gloat over me. (Ps. 22:14–17)

The next line gives it away: *They divide my garments among them and cast lots for my clothing.* This is an exact description of the crucifixion of Jesus, penned centuries before it took place.

Jesus Himself was convinced that the Psalms of David were written with specific reference to Him. In Psalm 110 David writes: *The LORD says to my Lord: "Sit at my right hand until I make your enemies a footstool for your feet."* In debate with the Pharisees, Jesus uses this text to discuss His identity as the promised Messiah.

> While the Pharisees were gathered together, Jesus asked them, "What do you think about the Christ? Whose son is he?"
> "The son of David," they replied.
> He said to them, "How is it then that David, speaking by the Spirit, calls him 'Lord'? For he says, 'The Lord said to my Lord: "Sit at my right hand until I put your enemies under your feet."'
> "If then David calls him 'Lord,' how can he be his son?" (Matt. 22:41–45)

The fact is, our Lord specifically identified the Psalms as central to the explanation of His life and work. Just before His ascension into heaven, while giving final directions to His apostles, He gave the Psalter a key role in their instruction:

> He said to them, "This is what I told you while I was still with you: Everything must be fulfilled that is written about me in the Law of Moses, the Prophets and the Psalms." (Luke 24:44)

No wonder, then, that Christians have been urged through the centuries to see the Psalter not only as the church's prayer book, but as Christ's prayer book as well. That is, as the written Word of God the Psalter is not only words *about* Jesus Christ but also words *from* Jesus Christ. When we pray the Psalms, it is our Lord Himself who prays with us.

This is why Christians do well to rely heavily on the Psalter for their private prayer. For in praying the Psalms, Christians pray the prayer of the one God and mediator between God and men, the man Christ Jesus, who always lives to make intercession for us.

When we pray the Psalms, we pray the very Word of God. We pray as we are taught to pray; we speak as we are spoken to. The Lord opens our lips, and our mouths show forth His praise. The prayers we pray in the Psalms are acceptable to God, for they are the prayers of the one in whom He delights, His holy Son. All psalmody is fundamentally therefore the prayer which Jesus Christ Himself ceaselessly prays through His church back to the Father. One ancient collect captures the thought exactly: "Come, pray in me the prayer I ought to pray."

I've discovered the enrichment the Psalter provides for personal prayer. For the Psalms are actually Christ's prayer. And in praying His words after Him, I find the peace and solace the Father longs to give. I commend this practice to you as well. The ancients had a saying for it—it sounds especially nice in their native tongue: *semper in ore psalmus, semper in corde Christus*. But we would probably prefer it in English: "always a psalm in the mouth, always Christ in the heart." How's that for a workable formula for private prayer?

PART 3: THE LITURGICAL SHAPE

With Heart and Mouth

In ore/in corde—"in mouth/in heart": these are the two focal points of prayer. Holy Scripture points out it is with the heart we believe and with the mouth we confess (Rom. 10:10). It's natural to speak that which we believe. When we do so in company with other believers, we confess—literally "say together"—the faith by which we live. Thus believing and speaking go together.

Prayer without faith is only empty repetition. Faith without prayer is like faith without love; it's on its way to extinction. When God says: "I love you," the child of God responds, "I love you, too." Our prayers are the "I love you, too" we speak to the Father, through the Son, in the Spirit. Prayer is the language of love.

Once we've said that, we recognize why prayer is deeper than mere words. Sometimes love is too profound for human language, after all. And that's the way it is with prayer as well. We use both heart and mouth in prayer. Occasionally the mouth falters, but the heart carries on. Thankfully God, who sees and hears in secret, understands the language of the heart.

> May the words of my mouth and the meditation of my heart
> be pleasing in your sight, O LORD, my Rock and my Redeemer.
> (Ps. 19:14)

Still, we would do well to keep our mouths linked with our hearts when we pray; private prayer works best when it is oral prayer. We all knew that when we were children. Our earliest prayers were spoken prayers. But somehow as we grow older we begin to think that such prayer is childish, that mature Christians should pray privately in their hearts and keep their mouths shut.

While the silent meditation of our heart is just as pleasing to God as the words of our mouth, we would do well to seek out places for private prayer where we can speak out loud. I'm convinced this is one reason Jesus advised His disciples to find a private location for prayer. We all need time to be alone in the presence of God, it is true. But we also need a place where we can pour out our heart before Him. And the best way to do that is by speaking out loud.

We're not pure spirits, after all; God has given us bodies as well as souls. And so when we as the children of God come to our

Father in heaven it's natural that we form our words with our lips as well as our hearts. Christians through the centuries have recognized that spoken prayer is effective prayer. Not only is it the most natural way for us to say what's on our heart, but it is also the natural way for our hearts to listen to the Word of God. *Faith comes from what is heard,* St. Paul wrote to the Romans (10:17 RSV). When we pray the Psalms or other portions of God's Word out loud, that Word strikes the eardrums as well as the heart. In that Word we draw strength, for when God speaks His Word we know we are no longer alone. And our hearts are brave again, for there is strength in His presence.

As it was at Sinai and in the public prayer of the congregation, so it is in our private prayer. God's Word comes first, then our response. Whenever the Lord speaks His Word, He summons His people to solemn assembly. The locations might be different, but the assembly is the same. Our liturgical life together and our liturgical life alone invite us into the presence of the same Holy Trinity. In His presence there is always one assembly, seen and unseen: the fellowship of angels, archangels, and the church in earth and heaven.

Body Language

Rather than being frustrated by the limitations of human senses, Christians through the ages have used them to enhance the practice of prayer. The fellowship of the church in heaven and earth is not seen with our eyes, for example, but appropriate statuary or artwork remind us that we are in the company of the faithful at all times. The presence of Jesus Christ with His church on earth is also invisible, but candlelight recalls the continual presence of the one who is the light of the world.

Watch people in animated conversation and you'll see how the human body is a useful tool for communication. The vocal cords never operate alone: arms move, fingers point, hands gesture, faces frown or radiate—all to move thoughts from one human heart to another. It works that way in prayer, too. Angels might be able to pray purely spiritual prayers, but human beings cannot. The fleshly body in which we live plays a role in our prayers.

Through the centuries Christians have used various postures for prayer, and all of them have some value. Sitting, for example, is the posture of learning, particularly appropriate for prayer which centers in meditation on God's Word. Standing is the posture of praise, an effective way to acknowledge the presence of God. Kneeling is the posture of humility, and for that reason alone has much to commend it, for genuine humility is hard to come by. When you confess your sins or bring your requests before God, it helps the heart to do so on your knees.

With a Voice of Singing

I promised you some thoughts on sung prayer. Music is one of the mysterious gifts of the Creator lavished on much of the created order. We've all been enchanted by the singing of birds, the purring of cats, the night songs of frogs and crickets, or the idle charm of the cicada's drone on a lazy summer day. Yet for some strange reason, Christians too easily overlook the value of sung prayer. Not so among the early Christians:

> Speak to one another with psalms, hymns and spiritual songs. Sing and make music in your heart to the Lord, always giving thanks to God the Father for everything, in the name of our Lord Jesus Christ. (Eph. 5:19–20)

Here we see that music is an effective vehicle for worship in both the public assembly and in private prayer. It serves as a witness to fellow Christians when we sing together in church, and it serves in private devotion to give voice to the meditation of our heart. It's time to reclaim this biblical and historic insight. For an entertainment mentality increasingly invades the worship of the church. It tempts us to view singing as a means of amusing ourselves and others.

The church's song is not a form of amusement. It is the way she gives voice on earth to the eternal praise which continually resounds in the courts of heaven. Christians have discovered through the ages that Psalms, hymns, and spiritual songs linger longer in the heart when sung than when spoken. With these songs on our lips, we move from public prayer in church to private prayer at home and then to daily work. The surroundings change; the song remains the same. And thus our life together, our life alone, and our life in the world becomes one great liturgy; from the Father through the Son in the Spirit and then back again.

In the worshiping congregation, hymns and other sung prayer are the means by which the diverse people in the assembly join their hearts into one voice. And in that one voice, their hearts are knit as well. Music has that special effect; it sometimes penetrates the heart when ordinary speech cannot. When we're alone at prayer, singing reminds us that we are not really alone. The unseen fellowship of the entire church is with us in that prayer; we hear it in the church's song placed on our lips to sing.

In either public or private, singing adds a third dimension to prayer. The mouth and the heart are involved in all prayer. But in singing the whole body gets to join in; the prayers and praises originating from the heart reverberate through muscle, bone, and cartilage, *always giving thanks to God the Father for everything, in the name of our Lord Jesus Christ.*

The Dry Times

Sometimes we don't feel like singing. That's not so bad; but sometimes we don't even feel like praying. What then? First off, it's important to remember to trust God over our feelings. Since He commands and invites us to pray, we should pray even when we don't feel like it. When the Psalms form the core of our personal prayer life, we find that the Word of God takes over where our feelings leave off. Better yet, we find our feelings being shaped by the Word of God. For God Himself provides our prayer in His Word. He speaks to us, and we answer in the words He teaches us.

The canticles of the public liturgy make excellent additions to private prayer. Besides praising God for the salvation He has given us, they remind us that we are a part of the believing community even when we are alone at our prayers.

This is where prayer books come in handy. They provide a framework for prayer that can see us through the thick and thin of our spiritual lives. The idea of using a prayer book might seem artificial at first, but there's a lot of wisdom in it. No one would seriously think about taking a trip through unknown territory without consulting a map. Why shouldn't we consult a spiritual guide when we set out to pray?

Please don't be concerned that the use of "set prayers" will stifle the prayers of your heart. Properly used, you'll find that prayer books actually prompt the heart to greater depth of prayer.

Don't worry; I'm not about to prescribe the book you use. Some of you may already have one on your shelf, some of you might dust off your catechism, others can utilize the devotional resources of your church's hymnal; you'll find no lack of resources if you look around. The best of these provide a rich mixture of resources: a lectionary of Bible readings for the church year, a selection of Psalms and hymns to match, and a smattering of classic collects or other prayers from Christians of other centuries.

Anyone who wants to get in shape physically gets set for a regimen. Physical conditioning demands discipline; muscles must be exercised in order to gain tone and strength. But muscles don't exercise themselves; bodies would rather sit than get up to run or lift weights. You know the old saying: "No pain, no gain." Why should it be any different with our spirits than with our bodies? Do you suppose we could use a framework for prayer? God seems to think so:

> For physical training is of some value, but godliness has value
> for all things, holding promise for both the present life and the life
> to come. (1 Tim. 4:8)

By now I hope you understand that there's more than one appropriate way to exercise your prayer muscles; there are many prayer disciplines available to you. But I'd like to recommend one that's had a long track record.

The Office of Prayer

For centuries Christians have spoken of a "Prayer Office"—and with good reason. By now you realize that prayer—even private prayer—is never a purely personal matter. For our prayers are not simply the haphazard thoughts of our head or the fleeting emotions of the moment. When we enter into prayer, whether private or public, we enter into the assembly of the firstborn, the entire company of believers on earth and in heaven. We enter something established; we enter an office of prayer.

We know that the people of God have always had prescribed times for prayer. In the Psalms we read, *Seven times a day I praise you for your righteous laws* (119:164). In the New Testament we read of Peter and John going up to the temple *at the time of prayer—at three in the afternoon* (Acts 3:1). Through the centuries Christians have developed many prayer services for different times of the day. These services lean heavily on the prayers recorded in the Bible itself: Psalms, canticles, and other Scripture verses. While these services are all useful, the most practical for most of us are the services of Morning and Evening Prayer, incorporating portions of the Matins and Vespers liturgies of the church. Together, these services have come to be known as the daily office. They work equally well for group prayer or private prayer. They might be just what you're looking for in your quest for effective prayer.

After all, when we want to do business, we go to an office, a place set apart for a special purpose. So also the prayer offices. When we go to our prayers we go with a purpose in our mind and on our heart. We mean business; this is serious business. This is God's business, the business of prayer. And when we enter that place of business we find that the one who holds office there is none other than Jesus Christ Himself:

> He holds his priesthood permanently, because He continues for ever. Consequently He is able for all time to save those who draw near to God through Him, since He always lives to make intercession for them. (Heb. 7:24–25 RSV)

Redeeming the Time

It's nice to know that Jesus is always praying for us, that He holds us always in His heart. For the truth is, we're not always thinking of Him. But with Christ and His church it is as it is in all matrimony; the marriage binds the partners together even when they're apart. Marriage is nurtured when the partners are together in body and heart, in conversation and intimate relations. But faithful husbands and wives remain married even through weeks and months of separation.

So it is with Christ and His church. We may not always be thinking of Him, but we exist in an estate of holy matrimony with our heavenly Husband. In the Divine Service He comes to us in intimate communion with His Holy Word and most sacred body and blood; in daily prayer we go to Him to speak the prayers and praises of our heart. His hand leads us and His love supports us day by day, for He delights in us. Therefore we live each day in the secular world as on sacred ground. For we are always in His presence, surrounded forever by His love. Redeemed by His blood, the church lives in this dying world in confidence and hope. For there is life in her glorious Lord.

Home Again

And so the liturgy goes on. As it is in the public prayers of the church, so it is in the private prayers of every Christian: the Father speaks to His children through the Son in the Spirit, and we pray back to Him what He has spoken in the Spirit through the Son. So the prayer, and so the song. The song and the prayer are one in origin and one in goal: from the most holy Trinity and back again. Thus once again God's children are back home where they belong—in His presence.

And in God's presence there is life, and peace for all His own.

9

Vocation: Liturgical Life in the World

And whatever you do, whether in word or deed, do it all in the name of the Lord Jesus, giving thanks to God the Father through him. (Col. 3:17)

It was time for review, and the production staff was nervous. The chief was a demanding boss. In fact, he had fired better men than they. But when the report came out, they were stunned by his evaluation: perfect scores across the board. "How can this be?" they asked. "We never performed that well for you."

"The King will reply, 'I tell you the truth, whatever you did for one of the least of these brothers of mine, you did for me.'"

Last but Not Least

We come now to the last chapter. Since it's about daily living, I suppose some would consider it the application chapter. But it's not. What I have to tell you about Christian vocation is not the end goal of the Christian faith; it's an extension of the Christian faith. This chapter is not the bottom line; it's only the tip of the iceberg. Underlying everything you and I do as Christians in this world are the incarnational foundation and sacramental focus described in the early chapters of this book. If those concepts are a bit fuzzy, it might be a good idea to stop right here to go back and skim through them. For the "bottom line" of the Christian's life in this world is the person and work of Jesus Christ Himself and what He continues to do still today through His Holy Word and Sacrament. In fact, the work of every Christian in this world is actually the work Jesus Christ is doing in and through that Christian.

161

Thanks, but No Thanks

I used to think the main motivation for Christian living was a thankful heart. Because of what Jesus did for me on His cross, I was supposed to thank Him by living a holy life. Of course it's true that the depth of Christ's saving love ought to move our heart to thanks and our lives to His service. *We love,* writes St. John, *because he first loved us* (1 John 4:19). But this love is more than skin deep. The love which prompts us to thankful service to others is not our own. It is the very love of Christ Himself, continually extended and dispensed to us in the proclamation of His Word and the administration of His Sacraments. Every deed of kindness, each work of love which you and I do for our fellow man is not our own. It is the work which Jesus Christ does, using us as His instruments. St. Paul describes it this way: *I have been crucified with Christ and I no longer live, but Christ lives in me. The life I live in the body, I live by faith in the Son of God, who loved me and gave himself for me* (Gal. 2:20).

Here's the real motivation for Christian living, and it involves a lot more than mere thankfulness. I discovered over and over again that a thankful heart wasn't enough to get me to lead a holy life. My problem was the same as Paul's: *For what I do is not the good I want to do; no, the evil I do not want to do—this I keep on doing* (Rom. 7:19). And that's your problem too; the problem we all have is our damned sinful nature: *the sinful mind is hostile to God. It does not submit to God's law, nor can it do so* (8:7). Remember, the sinful nature cannot be tamed or harnessed or brought under control; it must be killed. That's why the solution for Christian living is the same as the solution for sin: the forgiveness of sins.

All that the Father has in store for baptized believers on the Day of Judgment—indeed, all that the Father will give for all eternity in the world to come—rests on the forgiveness of our sins here in this world. Christians through the ages have confessed three blessed realities bestowed by God the Holy Spirit in His holy church: the forgiveness of sins, the resurrection of the body, and the life everlasting. This side of eternity, all three are hidden realities. One day we will see with risen eyes what we now believe. But not yet.

Here's where our sinful heart gets in the way. "What you see is what you get" is our motto; we prefer visible evidence and inner feeling to faith. We'd rather go with our own internal feelings than God's external promise. And so we construct the edifice of Christian living on the flimsy foundation of inner emotion. But it's a house made of cards. Thankfulness alone will not produce a holy life.

What we need for a right relationship with God our Father (justification) is exactly what we need for holy living (sanctification). These two columns of the Christian life rest on the same unseen foundation: the forgiveness of sins. Our entire relationship with both God and man always hinges on this one central reality. Faith toward God and love toward the neighbor find common nourishment in forgiveness through Jesus Christ our Lord.

Something happens to us when God forgives, you see. He wipes out our sin and declares us holy. The forgiveness of sins always brings with it a death and a resurrection—the death of the Old Adam and the resurrection of the new man in Christ. Living always in the forgiveness of our sins, we live in continual renewal in Christ. Here is solid footing for a new life. Holy people lead holy lives. No, we are not holy in and of ourselves, but the life we live as baptized believers is not our own. It is the life which Christ lives in us. And since it is Christ's life, it is a holy life.

The How-tos of Faith

We keep thinking the Christian life is a recipe we can whip up for ourselves. But it's not. Read the New Testament carefully, and you'll discover that the key to Christian living is the real presence of the living Christ with His church through His Holy Word and Sacrament. The best way to tell you what to do as a Christian is to tell you who you are in Christ. He will do the rest.

There are few how-tos in the New Testament. And with good reason. The center of the Christian life is Jesus Christ Himself. What is necessary for Christian living is to know who He is and who we are in Him. He is not simply our justification and redemption, but also our sanctification, according to St. Paul (1 Cor. 1:30). That is, Jesus Christ is Himself our holiness. The only "how-to" we need to live as Christians is how to find our life in Christ. He will take it from there.

Luther's catechism follows this New Testament pattern. "The lay-men's Bible," he called it—a condensation of the essence of the Christian faith and life. If you read it, you'll discover this catechism is no do-it-yourself manual. Rather, Christians are taught to pray and live as baptized children of God, to confess their sins and receive absolution from the mouth of their pastor as from Christ Himself, to eat and drink the body and blood of their Lord for forgiveness of sins, life, and salvation.

We'd rather know what we should do, yet God insists on telling us who we are. We are His precious children, created by the Father, redeemed by the Son, and sanctified by the Spirit. In our sin we are blind and dead and enemies of God. But in Christ we are holy. And holy people lead holy lives, each in his own situation.

We all have different duties to perform in this world, each according to our calling in life. But wherever God places us, there we live. And daily we are recreated in Him to be tools for the heavenly Father.

> We are God's workmanship, created in Christ Jesus to do good works, which God prepared in advance for us to do. (Eph. 2:10)

Since we are God's tools created in Christ Jesus, it is not we who live, but Christ who lives in us. That's why the life we live in the body we live always and entirely by faith in the Son of God, who loved us and gave Himself for us.

As it is in the public and private prayers of the church, so it is in the daily life of the Christian. All our works of service, all our prayers and all our praises have a common source and goal in the Holy Trinity. They all flow from the Father through the Son in the power of the Spirit and then back again in the Spirit through the Son to the Father.

And so all of life becomes liturgical living.

Our Spiritual Worship

That's why Jesus could tell His disciples that even a cup of cold water given in His name is a pleasing sacrifice to the Father. Even the most routine and ordinary actions of the Christian are done to the glory of God; and that's reality, not just pious talk. After all, how could it be otherwise? Can a zebra hide its stripes? Can a flame not give light? We are new creations in Christ Jesus, after all. Therefore the work we do in the name of Jesus is not our own. Jesus Christ Himself is the active agent in all our works of Christian service.

Of course we're not bumps on a log. We have work to do. Scripture urges: *continue to work out your salvation with fear and trembling* (Phil. 2:12). Yet where does our drive come from? Certainly not from our own willpower! . . . *for it is God who works in you to will and to act according to his good purpose* (2:13). Every good work we do is worked in us by God Himself. And that includes earthly actions, too—even the earthy ones.

There's no wedge, after all, between the spiritual and physical aspects of life. It may seem that way to us, but that's because we live in a fallen world. We experience reality in artificial slices; alternately physical, then spiritual. But in Christ wholeness is restored. Entering this physical world, He enclosed all the fullness of His divine nature in fragile infant flesh. Then by His bodily death and resurrection Christ rescued us from spiritual death.

It seems like a paradox, but it's wonderfully true: the earthly flesh and blood of Jesus Christ has purchased us a place in heavenly glory. Whatever else that may mean, it breaks down the wall we experience in this world. Now physical actions are shot through with spiritual reality. Among us it is as it was with Paul:

> I have been crucified with Christ and I no longer live, but Christ lives in me. The life I live in the body, I live by faith in the Son of God, who loved me and gave himself for me. (Gal. 2:20)

Thus the bodily activity of Christians is an expression of the presence of Christ in this world.

For the Christian, there's no dividing spiritual activity from physical actions in daily vocation. Through Christ's redeeming love, the actions of our bodies are just as acceptable to God as the thoughts and prayers of our minds. *I appeal to you therefore, brethren, by the mercies of God, to present your bodies as a living sacrifice, holy and acceptable to God, which is your spiritual worship* (Rom. 12:1 RSV).

You and I as sons and daughters of God our Father are created, redeemed, and sanctified to be partners with Him in this world. We are His tools and instruments in the lives of others. That goes for both sacred and secular activities. Every word and every action of every Christian is carried out by the Holy Trinity for the Holy Trinity. What's true for our prayers and praises also holds true for our works of Christian love and service—they are all liturgical offerings. They flow from our Triune God through us and then back again to Him.

Worship isn't just for Sundays. Every moment of every day the actions we do in and through Jesus Christ are liturgical offerings to our Father in heaven. We know these actions please Him because they flow from faith in Jesus Christ, who is the Father's delight. *"My beloved Son, with whom I am well pleased"* was the Father's verdict on Jesus (Matt. 3:17 RSV). And in Christ, we are the Father's pride and joy as well. Every little thing we do in this world by faith in Christ is a pleasant offering: to the Father, through the Son, in the Holy Spirit.

Now see what I mean? The Christian's daily vocation in this world is a liturgical life.

Eden Revisited

We seem to have lost touch with this reality. Work is often just that—work. And our hectic pace doesn't help much either. Most of us keep going faster and faster in our lives, yet we seem to be getting nowhere fast. Job satisfaction is rare among us. We call our daily work our "occupation," as if it's just a pastime or diversion. All too often, that's all we think of work, measuring its worth in terms of our paycheck alone. Rarely do we see our daily life for what it really is—a vocation, a calling from God.

It all started in Eden. Remember? God the Father not only provided Adam with food; He provided him with work. And it's clear from the text that along with that work came vocation: Adam was a partner with the Creator in providing for His creation: *The LORD God took the man and put him in the Garden of Eden to work it and take care of it* (Gen. 2:15). Adam's work was his calling.

But after his fall into sin, what had once been Adam's joyful privilege now became drudgery:

> To Adam he said, "Because you listened to your wife and ate from the tree about which I commanded you, 'You must not eat of

it,' Cursed is the ground because of you; through painful toil you will eat of it all the days of your life. It will produce thorns and thistles for you, and you will eat the plants of the field." (3:17–18)

Notice, however, that the rebellion of our first parents did not set aside the gift of the Creator or the honor of vocation. True enough, work now became "painful toil"; yet there was food as a result. Though they had to contend with thorns and thistles, still the Lord used the toil of His children to take care of His creation.

Through Christ, the second Adam, God the Father has removed the transgressions we all inherited from the first Adam. Baptized into Christ, we have put on Christ. *Therefore, if anyone is in Christ, he is a new creation; the old has gone, the new has come* (2 Cor. 5:17). As it was in the Garden of Eden, so it is with us, newly created by water and the Spirit. The Lord God not only invites us into His fellowship, He invites us into partnership with Him in this world. Every baptized child of God has a double calling: called into the holy Christian church and into a daily calling—a vocation—where he or she labors as a co-worker with God in the care of His creation.

Butcher, Baker, Candlestick Maker

We're tempted to think that God prefers some vocations over others; that some callings are more holy than others. In the middle ages people thought God preferred monastic orders to secular vocations. Still today some think pastors and other church workers are a bit holier than people engaged in more worldly occupations. But our work doesn't make us holy; we are sanctified by the grace of God. Baptized into Christ, we have put on Christ. He has taken our sin and given us His perfect righteousness. Like the Christians in Corinth, we are *sanctified in Christ Jesus, called to be saints together with all those who in every place call on the name of our Lord Jesus Christ, both their Lord and ours* (1 Cor. 1:2 RSV).

Saints are holy people. And you and I are "called to be saints." We are not holy in ourselves, but in Christ we are. Christ's blood and righteousness have removed our sin and shame and clothed us with His own holiness. In Jesus Christ our Lord we are truly holy people. Now holy people, you'll remember, do holy things. Therefore the most earthly work becomes a heavenly vocation, transformed by the presence of God. Thanks to Jesus Christ, whatever work we do in the shadow lands of this world is tinted with the bright colors of heaven.

Samuel's charge to Saul becomes our charter, too: *"do whatever your hand finds to do, for God is with you"* (1 Sam. 10:7). Butcher, baker, or candlestick maker; it doesn't matter. We don't have to wonder if our work in this world is "spiritual" enough. Christ's blood provides full payment for our sin; our relationship with God is already secured. That's a given. Now we can tend to the neighbor's need in perfect freedom.

Thus for the child of God in this world every occupation is a holy calling—holy with the presence of God. To be sure, some drudgery is connected with all work here in this fallen world. Yet among us it is the same as in Eden after the Fall. There is still honor in work, no matter how menial or tedious. Transformed by the presence of God, what others would consider only a job or occupation becomes a vocation, where the child of God labors in partnership with the Creator in the care of His creation.

Death and Life

Christian vocation brings true freedom, though at times it feels like bondage. I mentioned earlier that during Israel's long pilgrimage through the Sinai wilderness, they sometimes longed to return to bondage. The security of slavery seemed more attractive than the challenges of freedom. So it is with us; the unique duties of vocation seem threatening.

And genuine Christian vocation is threatening, when you stop and think about it. That's because it's built on the forgiveness of sins. The prison walls of sin provide perverse security, after all. The rattling chains of bondage seem strangely comforting to the sinful nature. Thus forgiveness of sins is sometimes intimidating. For as long as we are in this world, we're tempted to return to the comfort and security sin provides for the old Adam in us. To the old Adam, the freedom of sonship is a threat. The devil, a liar from the beginning, convinces us that freedom is bondage and bondage is freedom.

VOCATION: LITURGICAL LIFE IN THE WORLD

When our sinful nature is in control, the old Adam is perfectly content; going merrily on its selfish way, living for personal gain or pleasure. Such a life seems like freedom to the old Adam. There's just one problem: *Those controlled by the sinful nature cannot please God* (Rom. 8:8).

Thankfully, our Father in heaven intervenes through His Son in the power of His Spirit:

> You, however, are controlled not by the sinful nature but by the Spirit, if the Spirit of God lives in you. And if anyone does not have the Spirit of Christ, he does not belong to Christ. But if Christ is in you, your body is dead because of sin, yet your spirit is alive because of righteousness. (8:9–10)

Dead and alive; that's us. Dead in sin, yet simultaneously alive in Christ. Saints on the one hand—perfect and whole in the perfection of Jesus Christ—and yet at the very same time sinners, lost and condemned under the wrath of God. Dead and alive; sinner and saint at the same time.

That's why this side of heaven we're always dying to live. For as long as we are in this world, the Old Adam in us must go on dying, and the new man rising. God always kills so that He can make alive. He did it once in our Baptism, and He does it over and over again through contrition and repentance, as the Old Adam in us is drowned once more and the new man emerges to live before God in righteousness and purity forever.

No wonder Christian vocation often seems like bondage; for it too spells the death of the Old Adam. It's always a pleasure to serve our own needs and desires; but our heavenly Father leads us out of ourselves and into the service of others. Then personal pleasure takes a back seat to the demands of vocation. And in those demands, the Old Adam in us is drowned and dies over and over. A cantankerous boss can be quite demanding, but the cry of an infant in the night is no less insistent. While we might be more sympathetic to the infant than the boss, in both cases our selfish sinful heart is forced to sacrifice its own wants for the welfare of someone else—the Old Adam dies, in other words. And while the death of our Old Adam may hurt like hell, it's actually a gift from heaven.

Law and Gospel

Our heavenly Father attaches no strings to His love. His love for us doesn't depend on our love for others. Our relationship with the Father was established long ago, in the body and blood of His Son. Jesus Christ has erased all our sins and shouldered all our sorrows. Already now we have a solid relationship with our heavenly Father; there's no need to fret about it. That relationship doesn't depend on our love for Him, but on His love for us. It hinges on the Gospel of God, not the law of God. The Law tells us what to do. The Gospel tells what God has done to save us in Christ. The Gospel provides the power for vocation; the Law provides the direction.

Again the Old Adam betrays us. Our sinful nature would much rather hear Law than Gospel. The sinful nature is a seasoned do-it-yourselfer. The sinful nature likes to think it can earn God's favor. Our Old Adam prefers to base security with God the Father on His Law rather than His Gospel.

The Law, however, has nothing to say about our security with God in heaven. Rather, it lays down directives for Christian vocation in this world. "You shall love your neighbor as yourself," said Jesus. (Matt. 22:39 RSV). We can clearly see here in the Golden Rule that the goal of vocation is not holiness, but love. Holiness before God is a gift of the Gospel, already established by Christ. Love toward the neighbor is a requirement of the Law. Holiness before God is His free gift to us in His Son, received by faith. Therefore the Christian lives always in freedom and in bondage at the same time. In perfect freedom as far as the new man is concerned, but in bondage according to the Old Adam.

> You, my brothers, were called to be free. But do not use your freedom to indulge the sinful nature; rather, serve one another in love. The entire law is summed up in a single command: "Love your neighbor as yourself." (Gal. 5:13–14)

The new man needs no Law, but the Old Adam does. The new man is always alive in Christ, and therefore lives to love others. The Old Adam always lives for himself, and therefore is a self-love expert. Jesus Christ turns our inborn selfishness inside out: *"Love your neighbor as yourself."*

But our Lord is not a dictator; He is our savior. He is not the policeman of the soul; He is the doctor of the soul. What He tells us to do, He gives us to do. What He commands, He provides. Like the Good Samaritan who poured oil and wine into the wounds of a beaten man, our Lord Jesus brings us the medicine of heaven. Battered, beaten, and bruised, we are without hope and without life in this world. But our glorious Lord has rescued us. Not only at Calvary, but over and over again in His church He continues to lavishly dispense the healing medicine of His love. Pouring on the oil and wine of His Holy Word and Sacraments, He restores us to life and health and then says, *"Go and do likewise."* He is more than just an example for us; much more. Because He has loved us all the way to the cross and death, Jesus Christ provides us with more than directives; in His company there is the present reality of His love.

And you and I are in the company of our Lord in His church yet today. What Jesus promised His disciples the night of His betrayal is still true for us; our love for one another is in reality His love in action:

> "He who receives any one whom I send receives Me; and he who receives Me receives Him who sent Me. . . . A new commandment I give to you, that you love one another; even as I have loved you, that you also love one another." (John 13:20, 34 RSV)

God's Masks

You could say we are God's secret agents in this world. Not that there's anything hush-hush about it; it's the Father's express will that we should be agents of His love in Christ. Yet since God works in hidden ways, no one can see how He operates in this world. "Give us this day our daily bread," we pray. And God gives us a farmer, a miller, a baker, a trucker, a grocer. He provides good government, good weather, peace, health, self-control, good reputation, good friends, faithful neighbors—the list goes on and on. All to take care of the support and needs of the body.

The casual observer looks at daily life in this world and sees only industrial policy, economic theory, cultural anthropology, and political structures. But these are masks of God. Behind this human interplay, behind these ordinary structures of society, lies the extraordinary work of God. He uses ordinary people, motivated as they often are by selfish interests, to provide for the needs and wants of His whole creation.

Admittedly, only the eyes of faith can recognize these masks of God for what they are. But I leave it to you; does simple surface observation always tell the whole story? Can you fully appreciate a painting just by analyzing the brush strokes? Can you discover the real value of a pet on a dissection table? So what's really going on in society: is daily life just a blind jumble of impersonal forces, or is the hand of God behind it all? The inspired insight of the Psalmist sheds some light:

> The eyes of all look to you, and you give them their food at the proper time. You open your hand and satisfy the desires of every living thing. (Ps. 145:15–16)

This puts the butchers, bakers, and candlestick makers of this world in a whole different light. Every worldly vocation becomes an avenue for God the Father to provide for His creation. And that includes your vocation and mine. We are masks of God, behind which He Himself provides food and shelter, comfort and security for His children.

Hopefully this puts your daily work in a different light, too. It is not just your boss you're working for, after all. Payday is not your only motivation. You're not just a tiny functionary cog in great big impersonal wheel. You have a holy calling. Your work serves as a mask for the heavenly Father. The effort Christians put into daily work is effort well spent; it is faith in action. That's the way faith works: faith in Christ is always active in love for the neighbor. He carries on His work through us.

Jesus was always telling stories to illustrate the way things are between God and man. To teach His disciples about the final judgment, He told a series of stories about investment management, a wedding feast, etc. But when He wanted to clinch the point He did not tell stories; He told it straight, with just the facts of the matter. And those facts are quite striking:

> "When the Son of Man comes in his glory, and all the angels with him, he will sit on his throne in heavenly glory. All the nations will be gathered before him, and he will separate the people one from another as a shepherd separates the sheep from the

goats. He will put the sheep on his right and the goats on his left. Then the King will say to those on his right, 'Come, you who are blessed by my Father; take your inheritance, the kingdom prepared for you since the creation of the world. For I was hungry and you gave me something to eat, I was thirsty and you gave me something to drink, I was a stranger and you invited me in, I needed clothes and you clothed me, I was sick and you looked after me, I was in prison and you came to visit me.' Then the righteous will answer him, 'Lord, when did we see you hungry and feed you, or thirsty and give you something to drink? When did we see you a stranger and invite you in, or needing clothes and clothe you? When did we see you sick or in prison and go to visit you?' The King will reply, 'I tell you the truth, whatever you did for one of the least of these brothers of mine, you did for me.' " (Matt. 25:31–40)

Remarkable, isn't it? On the Last Day it will be clear that work done in the name of Jesus is actually done by Jesus Himself. Not only is Jesus fed, clothed, comforted, and visited in the actions of His followers, but Jesus Christ Himself is at work in those actions. When we feed the hungry, clothe the naked, tend the sick, visit the prisoners—in fact, even when we offer a cup of cold water in the name of Jesus—it is Christ Himself who is at work in those actions. We are masks of God, in other words, carrying out His work in this world.

That puts a whole new twist on Christian vocation. When you begin to see your daily routine from this angle, it's anything but routine! When you start to see your daily work as Christ's work in this world, it takes on a whole new dimension. While you're at work, Jesus Christ is at work pouring forth His love and care for others through what you do every day on the job.

That's Christian vocation in action. What better job could there be?

The Will of God

We spend so much of our lives searching for the ideal work. The grass always seems greener on the other side of the fence; there must be something better out there for us somewhere, we reason. At times we put it into a more spiritual framework; we go on a quest for the will of God. We wonder where God wants us to serve Him, not recognizing that He has put us where we are for a reason.

Saul's instructions would be good for us to remember: *"Do whatever your hand finds to do, for God is with you"* (1 Sam. 10:7). Certainly God's will guides our lives, and it is the Christian's goal to follow the will of God. But so often our search for God's will is limited to something in the future: where does God want me to head? We forget that God had a hand in placing us in our current situation. We don't have to wait for the future to be doing the will of God; we have a vocation to fulfill right now.

And in our daily routine we are masks for the heavenly Father; we are agents of Jesus Christ our Lord. Though we may not have achieved all we hope to achieve, we are partners right now with God. He is doing His work through us for the benefit of our neighbor. Why this endless search for something else? God's will applies not just to the future, but right now!

We keep wondering what God's will is, forgetting that His will is that everything be done to His glory. We keep looking for vocational direction, ignoring the direction that is before our very eyes. The tools of our trade and the responsibilities of our job provide us with direction, if we simply have the eyes to see and the ears to hear. The computer we work with every day, the hammer we pound, our tooling lathe or drill press, the goods we sell, the commodities we manage—all of these cry out to us: "Use me in the service of your neighbor as you would want your neighbor to serve you." This is faith at work. Faith in Christ is always active in love toward the neighbor.

God's will may be hidden, but it's no deep secret. We may have many different jobs during our lifetime, but only one vocation. Every baptized believer is a mask of God; through us He intends to preserve and protect His children in this world. This is His good and gracious will.

How's that for a holy calling?

Active and Passive

The Christian faith includes both believing and doing. This whole topic gets confusing sometimes. As Christian people we recognize that everything we have is a free gift. We cannot earn the Father's love by our actions; even our faith is a present from His Spirit. And yet we are called upon to be active in love. Which is God's part, we ask, and which is ours? Where does God's responsibility leave off and ours begin?

The same God who calls us into His family passively by faith calls us into active partnership with Him in vocation. Christian vocation channels the love of Christ into action in this world: *"You shall love your neighbor as yourself"* (RSV). God doesn't need our love, after all, but our neighbor does. And you can't keep Christian love in a box. Love always seeks the welfare of our neighbor, and that neighbor is a moving target. What he needs today he may not need tomorrow. That's why Christian vocation is never static; you can't define it in a rule book. Rather, it is defined by the cross of our Lord Jesus Christ: *"Love each other as I have loved you,"* He says (John 15:12). Thus love for the neighbor is the active choice of all who have been passively loved by Christ.

Here in this world we have free choice to perform works of love for our neighbor as partners with God in His creative work. Before his neighbor, the Christian is a doer of what the Father wants done in the world.

Before God, however, the Christian is not a doer, but a receiver. Love does not enter heaven; only faith enters heaven. Therefore in our relationship with God we check our vocation at the door; we leave behind all human love and works and rely solely and entirely on God's love in Christ.

We cannot choose eternal life; we receive it as a gift. There's no free will in heavenly matters; choice applies only in earthly matters. As a new man in Christ, the Christian chooses to love the neighbor with Christ's own love. But this love is not our own. Baptized into Christ, we have put on Christ. He is the one who extends His love through us to the neighbor.

Passive in faith, active in love. This is God's love in action; this is Christian vocation.

Saints and Sinners

As we are in Christ, so are we in this world. Both sinner and saint, both slave and free; all at the same time. Totally free in regard to everything below us, but absolutely bound in regard to things above. Passive and receptive toward God by faith, but active toward the neighbor by love.

We shouldn't be surprised, however, when Christian vocation doesn't always fill us with joy. For God approaches every one of us sinner/saints with both Law and Gospel. Since His call to vocation involves the death of the sinful nature, the prospect of God's judgment strikes fear in the heart of every sinner. Yet there is peace, joy, and freedom for all His saints, holy in His forgiveness and love.

We'd rather have it one way at a time. Sinner or saint, slave or free, Old Adam or new man, dead or alive. We keep thinking we're like Dr. Jekyll/Mr. Hyde: one person with multiple personalities that take over at different times. The ugly truth is that we're good and evil, saint and sinner, all at the same time. We know from bitter experience just what St. Paul was talking about: *I know that nothing good lives in me, that is, in my sinful nature. For I have the desire to do what is good, but I cannot carry it out* (Rom. 7:18).

This complicates things. What God has to demand from the Old Adam, the new man freely desires. What the Old Adam adamantly refuses to do in service of his neighbor, the new man eagerly wants to do. And try as we might, we can't sort things out; we don't know where the Old Adam leaves off and the new man begins. Like the recovering addicts we are, we start out on the path to freedom, but frequently retreat into bondage. Sickness and health jockey for position within us. We are at the same time sinner and saint.

As much as we hate to admit it, in Christian vocation it's impossible to sort out our motivations. We find resentment and joy, rebellion and love hopelessly intertwined in our hearts. Therefore as we have only one hope for justification, so we have only one hope for sanctification:

> What a wretched man I am! Who will rescue me from this body of death? Thanks be to God—through Jesus Christ our Lord! (Rom. 7:24–25)

I hope you see now why the forgiveness of sins is not just our initiation into the Christian life; it's our daily bread and butter. Let me repeat what I wrote at the beginning of this chapter: Faith toward God and love toward the neighbor find common nourishment in forgiveness through Jesus Christ our Lord.

Living Outside Ourselves

Want to know the secret to effective Christian vocation? It's well summed up in Luther's 16th century insight into the first-century Scriptures: the Christian always lives outside of himself—in Christ by faith and in the neighbor by love.

In the forgiveness of our sins you and I find freedom in vocation. To be sure, we will not finally be at home and at rest until we are at home in heaven's glory and at rest in God. But along the way there is rest already here in this world in the presence of God in the public liturgy, where God serves us with His Holy Word and Sacrament. And there is solace and comfort as we come into God's presence in prayer, which is our private liturgy.

As there is refuge for every exiled child of God in liturgical prayer, so there is comfort in liturgical living. For when we live each day by faith in Christ and by love in neighbor, we live outside ourselves. This means we find rest from our endless search for self-esteem. We live happy and content in the Father's love. He is well pleased with us, we know. For He is well pleased with His Son, and we live in Christ. In ourselves we are not perfect, but in Him we are!

More than that, we have the honor of being co-workers with our heavenly Father in providing for needs of the neighbor. No need to worry about our public image; we are agents of the Father's love. Despite what others may think of us, we find contentment within that love. Not only that, but we find integrity in our daily vocation. For through our daily work the love of the heavenly Father flows into this world, providing the sustenance and support our neighbor needs to live. Our hands, our feet, our thoughts and words and actions become channels for the Father's love. This is our vocation as Christians. What could be a richer privilege?

And so the three are all one: public liturgy and private prayer and daily vocation. The prayers and praises of heart and lips blend with the deeds of the body; all of them gifts received from the Father through the Son in the Spirit, then offered back again to the Father through the Son in the Spirit.

That's why Christian vocation is liturgical life in this world. It's the only way to live. For though we live in a dying world, we live in Christ. And in Him there is life forevermore.

In the name of the Father and of the Son and of the Holy Spirit. Amen.

The Last Word

There you have it. The Christian life as it's defined and shaped by Christ Himself through His Holy Word and Sacrament. In case you're wondering, this book doesn't represent the entire Christian faith. Some of you, I know, will wish I had added other topics—and perhaps many will wish I had left out some of what's included here.

Yet I've done the best I can with what I've been given. I am a preacher, remember; not a writer. And I leave to your judgment whether the holy mysteries of the faith have survived intact. Luther once remarked that the preacher never prays for forgiveness once he is done preaching; He leaves all in the hands of God, trusting that He will bring His Word to fruition. Our Lord reminds us that faith comes by hearing, after all.

And so the sermon is over; now the living begins.

"Okay," you respond. "Tell me what to do."

I'll try and resist the temptation to ask you to go back and read the book again. For according to St. John, the Christian life is not lived in word or speech only, but in deed and in truth (1 John 3:18).

You don't need more words; you need the Word.

For Jesus Christ, the Word of the Father made flesh, is Himself the center of the Christian life. That's why I cannot tell you what to do; I can only point you back to Him. I've suggested in these pages that there are three indispensable facets of the Christian life:

• The Incarnational Foundation
• The Sacramental Focus
• The Liturgical Shape

Having said that, I still haven't told you what to do. And I won't. For this is not a manual for Christian living, rather it's a travel guide for the Christian journey.

I know a manual would be more popular; people are always looking for rules for Christian living. Now don't misunderstand me; of course the holy Law of God prescribes the boundaries of the

Christian life. The child of God delights in that Law according to the new man. But our Old Adam delights in stepping out of those boundaries. And when we do, we get crushed again under the judgment of God. That's why the Law is never the way to find life in God: *law brings wrath* (Rom. 4:15).

Therefore as we look for power and direction for Christian living, we look not to the Law, but to the Gospel, which brings life. And that life is always the same. It is the life of Jesus Christ Himself, bought and paid for by His willing obedience to the Father and His bitter suffering and death for the life of the world.

Our living Lord is not locked up in the pages of history. Nor is He confined somewhere in heaven; the Father has *appointed him to be head over everything for the church, which is his body, the fullness of him who fills everything in every way* (Eph. 1:22–23). From His exalted throne in glory Jesus Christ continues to feed and nourish His church in His Holy Word and Sacrament. We are not left to muddle along here as best we can.

If there's one thing central to living the Christian life, it is the presence of our living Lord with His church. He fills our worship and our life as well. That's why we're always dying to live in this world. Daily dying to sin, yet daily rising in Christ to live a new life. Yet that life remains the same now and to all eternity.

For Jesus Christ is our life.

More than three years have come and gone since first I sat down to put words on paper. It's been a long journey, this pilgrimage of ours. And lots of words along the way. As I come to the last word, it is with mixed emotions. It has been thrilling to hike these paths with you; to point out the soaring peaks and majestic depths of the life that is in Jesus Christ. Yet I have a keen sense that I am only a very small guide in a very large landscape. I have listened as carefully as I could to those who have gone on ahead, and tried to convey their insights to you as faithfully as I'm able.

Yet when all is said and done, it is Christ who is our Guide. In fact, He is our path as well. On this pilgrimage Jesus Christ is Himself both the goal and the journey itself; I commend you to His care and keeping.

THE LAST WORD

As I write these final lines, the sun sets over the rolling Wisconsin countryside, casting a scarlet sheen over the wooded hillsides below. Chimney swifts circle in the twilight, their soft chatter the only sound in the stillness of the encroaching night. It is a setting conducive to peace of mind and heart.

But tomorrow is another day. And tomorrow I return to the life I live every day—a life, I suspect, not much different than yours; filled with both joy and struggle, heartache and gladness. And yet there will be peace in that life, the peace of the Lord Jesus Christ, which transcends all understanding.

If you don't know that peace, you should know that Christ grants it through the means He has appointed within the fellowship of His church. Seek out such fellowship, won't you? Find a pastor in whom you can confide and a church where you can be nourished in God's Holy Word and Sacrament. There is life in that Word and Sacrament, for there is life in Christ.

And His life is for you.

> Now to him who is able to do immeasurably more than all we ask or imagine, according to his power that is at work within us, to him be glory in the church and in Christ Jesus throughout all generations, for ever and ever! Amen. (Eph. 3:20–21)

A Reading List

The absence of footnotes in this book was deliberate, you may recall. You and I set out on this journey armed with Holy Scripture and very little else. It was my intention to travel light, without the encumbrances of scholarly notation ("academic luggage") which might get in the way of our mutual conversation.

It would be the height of arrogance, however, to pretend that the concepts and framework of this book are original with me. In the Christian church, every generation stands on the shoulders of those who've gone before. From that vantage point each Christian stands a bit taller, the better to glimpse the width and length and height and depth of the love of Christ.

Below are some of the giants who have lent me their shoulders. A few, as you can see, are contemporary giants. If you're interested in more reading, I'd encourage you to choose something from this list.

St. Athanasius on the Incarnation (London: A. R. Mowbray & Co., 1963). This is one of the most important books ever written. Over 16 centuries ago Athanasius stood very nearly alone against error inside the church and paganism outside it. Eminently readable and surprisingly contemporary in its application, this book eloquently outlines the timeless mysteries of the faith for our own troubled age.

Dietrich Bonhoeffer, *Life Together* (New York: Harper & Row, 1976). For several years prior to his execution in a Nazi prison camp, Dietrich Bonhoeffer directed an underground seminary in northern Germany. This book is a result of the communal life of Pastor Bonhoeffer and the 25 young men under his tutelage. It describes the implications of God's Word and Sacrament for worship, work, and daily life in the world, yet not of the world.

Dietrich Bonhoeffer, *Psalms: The Prayer Book of the Bible* (Minneapolis: Augsburg Publishing House, 1974). This little book, born of struggle (see above), is concise in format and devotional in tone. It provides invaluable direction for the use of Psalms in daily prayer.

A READING LIST

Bo Giertz, *The Hammer of God* (Minneapolis: Augsburg Publishing House, 1973), translated by Clifford A. Nelson. A leader in the Church of Sweden, Bishop Giertz weaves an engaging tale of three generations of pastors and parishioners in the same rural Swedish congregation. Each generation of Christians is threatened by a different heresy—whether rationalistic, pietistic, or modernistic. The same rock solid foundation provides correction and vitality throughout: the message of Jesus Christ and Him crucified. This book provides useful handles for modern Christians on faith/life issues and sacramental living.

Os Guinness, *Dining with the Devil: The Megachurch Movement Flirts with Modernity* (Grand Rapids: Baker Book House, 1993). I came upon this book after I was finished writing; I include it here because it so well describes the seduction of the church in our time. Long ago Geoffrey Chaucer warned that Christians who dine with the devil had better use a very long spoon. Guinness updates that warning. His book is a friendly critique of American Evangelicalism and its fascination with current culture. "By all means dine at the table of modernity," he concludes, "but in God's name keep your spoons long."

Adolf Köberle, *The Quest for Holiness* (Minneapolis: Augsburg Publishing House, 1936). In this classic discourse on the holy life, Köberle shows the sharp difference between justification and sanctification and at the same time illuminates their underlying unity in the person and work of Jesus Christ.

Walther von Loewenich, *Luther's Theology of the Cross* (Minneapolis: Augsburg Publishing House, 1982). Luther's theology takes death seriously. He saw the crucified God at the heart of the entire Christian faith and life. In his classic study, von Loewenich explores this "theology of the cross," as Luther called it. Sometimes difficult reading, the book nevertheless effectively examines this theme and its significance in Reformation times and for the daily life of Christians today.

Eugene Peterson, *Answering God: The Psalms as Tools for Prayer* (New York: Harper & Row, 1989). Eugene Peterson, a Presbyterian minister, provides us with a window into God's own prayer book, the Psalms. Unlocking the cultural background of the Psalms, he shows how God gives voice to His contemporary church through these ancient songs. Not simply historical investigation, this book abounds in application, e.g., "Prayer by its very nature is answering speech." "When we pray, we immerse ourselves in the living presence of God."

Hermann Sasse, *We Confess* series [I. Jesus Christ: II. The Sacraments; III. The Church], (St. Louis: Concordia Publishing House, 1985), translated by Norman Nagel. Hermann Sasse, an important Lutheran theologian of the 20th Century, was active in the "Confessing Church" movement which arose in Germany in opposition to the Nazi regime. These volumes are collections of essays Sasse wrote before, during, and after the Second World War for the benefit of parish pastors. Though the topics range widely, the church's confession over against heresy, apostasy, and tyranny comes through eloquently.

Alexander Schmemann, *For the Life of the World* (Crestwood, NY: St. Vladimir's Seminary Press, 1988). This book by the late dean of St. Vladimir's Seminary is a frank apologetic for the Orthodox Church. It holds important gems, however, for Christians in other sacramental churches. Matters such as worship, work, and personal piety come into clear focus through a Christo-centric lens.

Wilhelm Stählin, *The Mystery of God* (St. Louis: Concordia Publishing House, 1964), translated by Henry Horn. Wilhelm Stählin, late Bishop of Oldenburg, Germany, set out to describe the "biblical concept of mystery as the presence of the hidden God in the world." He shows how the life of the church in this world—indeed the life of every Christian—is shaped by the presence of the Holy Trinity in His Word and Sacrament. This book, long out of print, is well worth hunting for simply because of its eloquent description of the classic Lutheran sacramental prepositions: in, with, and under.

Gustaf Wingren, *Luther on Vocation* (Philadelphia: Fortress Press, 1957), translated by Carl S. Rasmussen. Here's the book for anyone who has ever struggled with alienation in the workplace or burnout on the job. Scholarly in tone, yet thoroughly practical in its application, it distills key writings of Martin Luther on daily life as Christian vocation. Laced with quotes in the Reformer's own vigorous prose, this book pulls long-forgotten truths into the lively arena of the everyday world.